DRINKING WITH DICKENS

My magnificent order at the public-house

DRINKING
WITH
DICKENS

being a light-hearted sketch
by
CEDRIC DICKENS
great-grandson of Charles Dickens

FACSIMILE OF CHARLES DICKENS' BOOK-PLATE

Elvendon Press
Goring-on-Thames   England
Hippocrene Books Inc.
New York

At the CATASH

First published 1980 by Cedric Dickens
This edition published September 1983 by Elvendon Press,
Goring-on-Thames, England, and Hippocrene Books Inc,
New York

ISBN 0 906 552 24 9   (Great Britain)
ISBN 0-88254-879-4   (United States)

Designed by François de Mauny MSIAD
Photoset by Carlton Photosetting Ltd
Printed and bound in Great Britain by Butler & Tanner Ltd,
Frome and London

Contents

To
John Greaves
late Hon. Secretary to
the Dickens Fellowship

"Will you permit me to have the pleasure, sir?"

It would be impossible to express my appreciation to all those who have helped me with this book.

Let me say a simple thank you to all my friends all over the world, especially to the Dickens Fellowship branches in Adelaide, Bath, Boulogne, Broadstairs, Haarlem and Philadelphia: to David Parker, curator of the Dickens House Museum at 48 Doughty Street, London, and the helpful and amiable staff there: to Alan Watts, Hon. Secretary of the Dickens Fellowship – a budding Mr Pickwick, swellin' wisibly – for putting me right in so many ways: to my brother, Harry, and his gorgeous and gifted staff, for their ideas and help in the preparation of the manuscript: to Messrs Hodder & Stoughton for permission to use Frank Reynold's sublime Mr Micawber and Young David who grace the back cover: to the Henry W and Albert A Berg Collection, The New York Public Library, Astor, Lenox and Tilden Foundations and the Pilgrim Edition of the Letters of Charles Dickens for permission to copy the letter to John Noble on page 64: to Michael Saunders-Watson of Rockingham Castle for allowing me to copy the original recipe, "Moonbeams": to Ainsley Johnson for dotting my Ps and Qs so relentlessly; but mostly to Elizabeth, my darling wife, for her encouragement, and especially for drinking unflinchingly the many potent potions included in this book, for making me discard the more vicious, for doing most of my share of the gardening and making my life so very happy.

"What does my noble captain drink – is it brandy, rum, usquebaugh? Is it soaked gunpowder, or blazing oil? Give it a name, heart of oak, and we'd get it for you, if it was wine from a bishop's cellar, or melted gold from King George's mint."

God bless you, everyone.

Cedric Dickens
Somerset
Friday 13 June 1980

Christmas Eve at Mr Wardle's

Introduction

Maurice McCullum, young, enthusiastic, professor of English Literature at the College of the Pacific, Stockton, California, stayed with us in January. Snow was on the ground and it was conducive to spending the time browsing over Dickensian recipes and, perchance, to taste here and there.

The more he tasted the more enthusiastic he became. It was, I think, over a steaming bowl of Bishop that he hammered the table and made me promise to record some of the recipes handed down to me or collected from my friends all over the world. Next morning it still seemed a good idea - the more so when I realized that nobody seems to have milked the fertile pages of my great-grandfather's works and letters to gather some of the glorious drinks found there.

Yes, Charles Dickens was my great-grandfather, and how lucky I am! Even today, more than a hundred years after his death, the magic of his name opens all kinds of unsuspecting doors - not only in London or England, but all over the world.

People love talking about him, possibly because he was the champion of the ordinary man, and because he wrote rattling good stories about characters who live today, characters ripe for television. Take for instance A Christmas Carol, which so often appears at Christmastide and surely helps to give that extra happiness so necessary at that time of the year: *"I will honour Christmas in my heart, and try to keep it all the year."* The family round the fireside - the shadowy light of candles and flickering firelight, the warmth and intimacy of the family circle, and the punch bowl on the hearth. Yes, even poor Bob Cratchit, earning a

To make Ginger = Beer.

To 9 Gallons of Water put
24 Pounds of Lump Sugar
3/4 of a Pound of White Raw
Ginger well bruised, and the
rind of 8 large Lemons pared
very thin, boil it half an
hour, let it stand till Milk
warm, then put it in your
Cask, with the Juice of the
Lemons, and 2 Pounds of
Sun Raisins chopped, and 3
or 4 Table Spoonsful of New
Yeast. Stir it every day,
at the Bung Hole, for 10
days, then if it is done
working, put in half an
Ounce of Isinglass & a

Quart of Brandy — Stop it
close, and in 8 or 10
weeks it will be ready to
bottle.
The Raisins & Lemon Peel
should be put into Muslin
Bags.

Auntie Georgie's Recipe for Ginger Beer

pittance, compounded his punch at Christmas. The Bob Cratchits, and indeed all the characters of Dickens' world, live on in our imagination and in fact still exist.

Once I was being driven in London by a taxi driver who was the double of Tony Weller, the great coachman in Pickwick Papers, and the father of Sam. It was Tony Weller who gave Mr Pickwick the cure for gout: *"Jist you marry a widder as has got a good loud woice, with a decent notion of usin' it, and you'll never have the gout again."*

We began talking and I pointed out The Six Jolly Fellowship Porters, the public-house bulging out with a dropsical air over the river Thames. In the days of my great-grandfather the door posts bore an inscription proclaiming it "The Early Purl House". That very friendly Dickensian taxi driver introduced me to my first taste of Purl.

In New Orleans I was taken by a benevolent Mr Wardle to the Pickwick Club. This was the first of a long line of Pickwick Clubs all over the world; it was founded in Charles Dickens' lifetime. There I was given a Mint Julep. A Mr Simmery in New York mixed a Dry Martini for me; this was sweet in comparison with the one a Captain Swosser gave me recently in Philadelphia.

Charles Dickens, his characters, the Christmas of Dickens, and the ever present punch bowl are all symbolised for me by a little book lying on my desk as I now write. Dated 1859, it is a penny note book of drink recipes kept by "Auntie Georgie" – Georgina Hogarth – when she was looking after the younger children at Gads Hill, Charles Dickens' last home. It starts with a recipe for Ginger Beer, a teetotal drink, which calls for a quart of brandy!

Then there is the catalogue of the Gads Hill sale after Charles Dickens died, which shows the contents of the cellar at that time. It would be large by today's standards, but must have been conservative then. (See Appendix 2).

There are also recipes which have been handed down through the mists of time – in the case of Milk Punch, from Mr Robert Sawyer, late Nockemorf, himself. One practically lethal potion comes from a very old Australian friend, Edmund Gosse, who when travelling to

England concocted it with the purser of the ship. To be fair to him, he was very much younger in those days.

Many of the drinks are medicinal and of course this is right: alcohol judiciously taken is the staff of life. Moderation is the key to happiness in so many things. My grandfather, Sir Henry Dickens, affectionately known as Pupsey, remembers his father as being abstemious in his habits, although there was much in his books concerning good cheer and plentiful libations – especially in Pickwick Papers which he started when just twenty-four years old.

Pupsey too was abstemious in his habits. He ended a successful career at the Bar as Common Serjeant, the City of London's own judge, and had to go to many a City dinner. He used to drink a bottle of champagne whilst dressing for dinner, and considered my parents decadent because they shared a bottle. I don't remember if he suffered in the morning, although he did on occasions complain of "crinkly toes" in bed. Many years later I discovered what he meant by crinkly toes and even remembered the prevention and cure. He was indeed a great man and I only wish I had been old enough, and interested enough, to pump him about his famous father. He must have known him well, being twenty-one at the time of his death.

Pupsey came on holiday with my father Pip (named after Philip Pirrip), and me on a banana boat in 1931. He savoured the glorious Green Swizzle in Barbados and Rum Punch on the shores of the Pacific, having taken his first flight at the age of eighty-two, over the Panama Canal. I remember he kept his pocket watch at Greenwich Mean Time because it belonged to his father and was not to be tinkered with. He infuriated everyone by wandering round the deck complaining that the meals were late.

On our first night out of port he witnessed young Siegert, great-grandson of the founder of the Angostura Bitters firm, uphold the honour of the company. Two old buffers at the next table were discussing the demerits of Angostura – how, if a drop falls onto a piece of raw meat, it will eat its way through in no time. Robert Siegert went to the bar, poured a wine glass half full of the Bitters and took it over to their table: "I don't normally eavesdrop,

Mrs Gamp proposes a Toast

Gentlemen; but I couldn't help overhearing your remarks about this drink. It is pure, Gentlemen: it is a tonic. I was brought up on it. Your health."

To this day I remember their astonishment as he drained the glass, and mine when they called for the bottle and perused that wonderful label. In those days it even included a table showing the number of drops to put into baby's bottle at various weeks. They were converted, as was I. It has saved my life on many occasions: a tablespoon in a tumbler of soda water has a sobering effect, and, taken in the morning, cures depression.

In the same way, an old surgeon friend of Pip, suspecting he might over-indulge, used to leave at his bedside a large tumbler three-quarters full of water, with a tablespoon full of "Enos" balanced on top and three aspirins alongside. How easy to knock the spoon into the glass, take the pills and drink. He never suffered from a hangover.

Even plain soda water helps. *When Mr Pickwick awoke, late the next morning, he had a confused recollection of having, severally and confidentially, invited somewhere about five-and-forty people to dine with him at the George and Vulture, the very first time they came to London; which Mr Pickwick rightly considered a pretty certain indication of his having taken something besides exercise, on the previous night.* Next morning he *evinced an unusual attachment to silence and soda-water.*

So, with that preventative advice under your belt, let us savour some of the delights of Pickwick and other potions.

But remember Sarah Gamp's admonition: *"Drink fair, wotever you do!"*

Setting the Scene

In England betwen 1825 and 1828 the whole licensing system was being overhauled and consolidated. The Free Trade movement was gaining momentum and in 1830 the then Prime Minister, the Duke of Wellington, removed the tax from beer and cider. How incredible! There were apparently two motives for this – to loosen the "tied house" system, where brewers owned public-houses, and to try to reduce the consumption of gin. It did have a marginal effect on the latter.

But the immediate result was the opening of a swarm of "Tom and Jerry" shops or "Tiddlywinks". Within six months over 24,000 new beer sellers had paid their fee of two guineas. Drunkenness became even more rife, the British and Foreign Temperance Society was founded and the House of Commons set up a committee on drunkenness which reported in 1834.

Meanwhile, established public-houses, which sold spirits and wine as well as beer, tried to retain their clients. Many turned themselves into "Gin Palaces" – dazzling places of plate glass, and a passion for gas-lights and gilding.

Such was the scene in 1832 when Charles Dickens entered the gallery as a Parliamentary reporter at the age of twenty. At the end of 1833 his first short story was printed in the "Monthly Magazine", and in August 1834 he joined the staff of The Morning Chronicle. Six months later The Evening Chronicle was founded, with a Scottish friend, George Hogarth, as editor. The first number included a sketch by Dickens; more followed over the next seventeen months. In 1836 he began Pickwick Papers in monthly parts and

The Maypole

married Catherine, George Hogarth's eldest daughter. Six months later he was famous.

His first two books, Sketches by Boz and Pickwick Papers, provide most of his drinking scenes. And why not? He was young and life was good.

A Select Committee had reported glowingly on Gin Palaces; but Dickens wasn't as enthusiastic in his sketch, "Gin Shops". He was, however, a lover of taverns and public houses – those which resisted the temptation to modernise and become garish in order to sell spirits. In my great-grandfather's works, references to "snug" inns and taverns are legion. Let me remind you of just a few: *All bars are snug places, but the Maypole's was the snuggest, cosiest, and completest bar that ever the wit of man devised. Such amazing bottles in old oaken pigeon-holes; such gleaming tankards dangling from pegs at about the same inclination as thirsty men would hold them to their lips; such sturdy little Dutch kegs ranged in rows on shelves; so many lemons hanging in separate nets, and forming the fragrant grove – suggestive, with goodly loaves of snowy sugar stowed away hard by, of punch, idealised beyond all mortal knowledge.*

CHRISTMAS PUNCH

Peel into a very strong common basin (which may be broken, in case of accident, without damage to the owner's peace or pocket) the rinds of three lemons, cut very thin, and with as little as possible of the white coating between the peel and the fruit, attached. Add a double-handful of lump sugar (good measure), a pint of good old rum and a large wine glass full of brandy – if it be not a large claret glass, say two. Set this on fire, by filling a warm silver spoon with the spirit, lighting the contents at a wax taper and pouring them gently in. Let it burn three or four minutes at least, stirring it from time to time. Then extinguish it by covering the basin with a tray, which will immediately put out the flame. Then squeeze in the juice of the three lemons, and add a quart of *boiling* water. Stir the whole well, cover it up for five minutes, and stir again. At this crisis (having skimmed off the lemon pips with a spoon) you may taste. If not sweet enough, add sugar to you liking, but observe that it will be a *little* sweeter presently. Pour the whole into a jug, tie a leather or coarse cloth over the top, so as to exclude the air completely, and stand it in a hot oven ten minutes, or on a hot stove one quarter of an hour. Keep it until it comes to table in a warm place near the fire, but not too hot. If it be intended to stand three or four hours take half the lemon peel out, or it will acquire a bitter taste. The same punch allowed to grow cool by degrees, and then iced, is delicious. It requires less sugar when made for this purpose. If you wish to produce it bright, strain it into bottles through silk.
To make three pints of punch.   18 January 1847
Note – With modern spirit extinguish flames after only one minute.

George Cruikshank

Scotland Yard

The Six Jolly Fellowship Porters is still there, *long settled down into a state of hale infirmity.* It was an old tavern which *had outlasted, and clearly would yet outlast, many a better-trimmed building, many a sprucer public house,* whose bar softened the *breast and was girt in by corpulent little casks and by the polite beer-pulls that made low bows when customers were served with beer.*

The Marquis of Granby *was quite a model of a roadside public-house of the better class – just large enough to be convenient, and small enough to be snug. The bar window displayed a choice selection of geranium plants, and a well-dusted row of spirit phials. The open shutters bore a variety of golden inscriptions, eulogistic of good beds and neat wines; and the choice group of countrymen and hostlers lounging about the stable-door and horse-trough, afforded presumptive proof of the excellent quality of the ale and spirits which were sold within.*

We must not forget the George and Vulture, George Yard, Lombard Street, City, Mr Pickwick's favourite hostelrie with its *very good, old-fashioned, and comfortable quarters.*

The choisest spot in all Scotland Yard was the old public house in the corner. Here, in a dark wainscoted room of ancient appearance, cheered by the glow of a mighty fire and decorated with an enormous clock, whereof the face was white, and the figures black, sat the lusty coalheavers, quaffing large draughts of Barclay's best, and puffing forth volumes of smoke.

Until 1839 public houses had to close only during divine service on Sunday. Thereafter this was extended from midnight on Saturday to midday on Sunday, producing a wonderful effect on Public Order. That scoundrel, Noah Claypole, and his wife, spent Sunday mornings taking turns to faint near public houses – so as to be revived with brandy, a whole threepenny-worth, in order to be able to inform against the charitable publican.

The pub is a very English institution: it is the centre of village life, and I am delighted to say that thousands still survive to provide an atmosphere which encourages good fellowship, conversation and happiness. In my "local", politics are normally barred: *"My faith in the people governing, is, on the whole, infinitessimal; my faith in The People governed, is, on the whole illimitable".*

However, it is spirits which demonstrate the greatest change in drinking habits. In those days, spirits were a deal stronger and nastier than they are today; this accounts for the popularity of mixing them with cordials, heating them or even burning off the raw spirit. Gin was cheap and the tipple of the poor. Brandy was the drink of the rich, and rum seems to have been imbibed by most – reaching the upper classes in the form of punch. Whisky in England was a rarity. But we will see this in more detail in the following chapters.

"Pray give your orders, gen'l'men – pray give your orders", and

First Appearance of Mr Samuel Weller, 23rd May 1827

demands for 'goes' of gin and 'goes' of brandy, and pints of stout, and cigars of peculiar mildness, are vociferously made from all parts of the room.

It is still possible to recreate those days if you have a good imagination. I walk my friends around Borough High Street and show them an old coaching inn, and the site of The White Hart where Mr Pickwick met Sam Weller on that fateful day – 23 May 1827. There are the sites of two prisons (one, the Marshalsea prison for debt, in which my great great-grandfather was incarcerated); Little Dorrit's church where she was christened, where she slept the night in the crypt (when she was too late to get back into the Marshalsea prison), and where she was married from; a dock in which London's last suspected witch was ducked; and many other historical places.

There is nothing in the world so irresistibly contagious as laughter and good-humour. How much better indeed the world would be if everyone laughed.

So, with alacrity, let us explore the heart of the matter – the drinks.

A Background to Drinking 1830-1870

BEER

There was no beer in the Gads Hill sale which isn't surprising. It would have been kept in barrels, but vanished between Charles Dickens' death and the sale. Certainly the servants would have had their daily ration from the barrels which were probably locked in the butler's pantry. The pantry faced north and the beer would pour clear and cool, unlike the beer we drank when I was a student at Cambridge.

We kept the beer in our hot and smoky sitting-room. To counter the atmosphere, the first man back after the holidays was responsible for getting in two small barrels, covering them with damp cloths on which he sowed cress. Three days later mustard seed was added and allowed to germinate. At this juncture a barrel was spiled and two days later tapped. Three more days and a quarter of a pint was drawn and thrown away. Invitations were then issued to particular friends to join a select first-of-the-term party – the girls to eat mustard and cress sandwiches, the men to drink the clearest, coolest glass of amber ale ever drawn – ale fit for young Charles himself. The roots of the mustard and cress keep the beer at a constant 56° farenheit however hot and smoky the room.

In winter we mulled ale – a stronger beer.

He was none of your flippant young fellows, who would call for a tankard of mulled ale, and make themselves as much at home as if they had ordered a hogshead of wine.

The Friendly Waiter and I

MULLED ALE	*1 Muller full of strong ale*
	1 tablespoon sugar
	pinch ground cloves
	pinch nutmeg
	pinch ginger
	1 glass brandy or rum

Put the muller with the ale, sugar and spices into the fire allowing those contents to heat (but not boil). Add the spirit and pour into warmed glasses adding more sugar if needed.

Try 2 oz of the spirit in the glass, pouring the hot beer on top.

Young David Copperfield, on his way from Blunderstone to school in London, was given dinner in the coaching inn at Yarmouth. The waiter hovered, making it difficult for the boy to handle his knife and fork. After watching him into the second chop, he said:

"There's half a pint of ale for you. Will you have it now?"

I thanked him and said, "Yes." Upon which he poured it out of a jug into a large tumbler, and held it up against the light, and made it look beautiful.

"My eye!" he said. "It seems a good deal, don't it?"

"It does seem a good deal," I answered with a smile. For it was quite delightful to me to find him so pleasant. He was a twinkling-eyed, pimple-faced man, with his hair standing upright all over his head; and as he stood with one arm a-kimbo, holding up the glass to the light with the other hand, he looked quite friendly.

"There was a gentleman here yesterday," he said – "a stout gentleman, by the name of Topsawyer – perhaps you know him?"

"No," I said, "I don't think –"

"In breeches and gaiters, broad brimmed hat, grey coat, speckled choker," said the waiter.

"No," I said bashfully, "I haven't the pleasure –"

"He came in here," said the waiter, looking at the light through the tumbler, "ordered a glass of this ale – WOULD order it – I told him not – drank it, and fell dead. It was too old for him. It oughtn't to be drawn; That's the fact."

I was very much shocked to hear of this melancholy accident, and said that I thought I had better have some water.

"Why, you see," said the waiter, still looking at the light through the tumbler, with one of his eyes shut up, "our people don't like things being ordered and left. It offends 'em. But I'll drink it if you like. I'm used to it, and use is everything. I don't think it'll hurt me, if I throw my head back, and take if off quick. Shall I?"

I replied that he would much oblige me by drinking it, if he thought he could do it safely, but by no means otherwise. When he did throw his head back, and take it off quick, I had a horrible fear, I confess, of seeing him meet the fate of the lamented Mr Topsawyer, and fall lifeless on the carpet. But it didn't hurt him. On the contrary, I thought he seemed the fresher for it.

"What have we got here?" he said, putting a fork into my dish. "Not chops?"

"Chops," I said.

"Lord bless my soul!" he exclaimed, "I didn't know they were chops. Why a chop's the very thing to take the head off the bad effects of that beer! Ain't it lucky?"

And he proceeded to demolish the chops and the pudding too.

Later, one hot evening in London, David went into a bar of a public house (see frontispiece) – there was no age limit to drinking in bars in those days. It was to celebrate something; he couldn't remember what. Maybe it was his birthday.

"What is your best – your VERY BEST – ale a glass?"

"Twopence-halfpenny," says the landlord, "is the price of the Genuine Stunning ale."

"Then," says I, producing the money, "just draw me a glass of the Genuine Stunning, if you please, with a good head to it."

The landlord looked at me in return over the bar, from head to foot, with a strange smile on his face; and instead of drawing the beer, looked round the screen and said something to his wife. She came out from behind it, with her work in her hand, and joined him in surveying me. Here we stand, all three, before me now. The landlord in his shirtsleeves, leaning against the bar window-frame; his wife looking over the little half-door; and I, in some confusion, looking up at them from outside the partition. They asked me a good many questions; as, what my name was, how old I was, where I lived, how I was employed, and how I came there. To all of which, that I might commit nobody, I invented, I am afraid, appropriate answers. They served me with ale, though I suspect it was not the Genuine Stunning: and the landlord's wife, opening the little half-door of the bar, and bending down, gave me my money back, and gave me a kiss that was half admiring, and half compassionate, but all womanly and good, I am sure.

Nowadays the number of people brewing their own beer increases as the price escalates. It is easy and the resulting drink is pure. A friend in Somerset has been brewing for fifteen years and has never since caught a cold, although very prone to them before. He is quite convinced that his immunity comes with his beer.

BEER	*2 oz hops*
	2oz crystal malt
	2½ lb malt extract
	3 lb brown sugar
	1 teaspoon salt
	castor sugar
	¾ oz dried yeast

Boil the hops and crystal malt (slightly cracked in a coffee grinder) in a butter muslin bag for half an hour in one gallon of water.

Empty into a clean container and add malt extract, sugar and salt.

Mix thoroughly and add four gallons of water to bring temperature to between 70° and 80°F.

Dissolve one teaspoon sugar in half pint warm water and stir in three quarters oz dried yeast. When well creamed add to the container, cover and leave in warm room.

Stir occasionally for the first two days. Fermentation will stop in about four or five days. Then syphon into clean screw-top bottles to which half teaspoon sugar has been added. Don't fill too full. Screw tightly and leave in room temperature for a week. Store in cool place and leave at least another week before drinking – longer if possible.

Decant into large jug leaving sediment in bottle.

More hops for greater bitterness. More malt for added body, flavour and strength, and more sugar gives even more strength.

Try a five gallon polythene bag with a tap for storage instead of bottles. The beer will keep well for a long time.

There was also a goodly jug of well-browned clay, fashioned into the form of an old gentleman, atop of whose bald head was a fine white froth answering to his wig, indicative, beyond dispute of sparkling home-brewed ale.

My experiments over the same period have given me enormous fun, and the beer is certainly a grand antidote to sleeplessness. They do say, although I haven't tried it, that a pillow filled with hops is guaranteed to give deep and peaceful sleep.

However I did once drink a glass of home-made porter with similar results. Porter was so named because it was drunk by the market porters. Dog's Nose should be made with it. Mr Walker, a convert to the Brick Lane branch of the United Grand Junction Ebenezer Temperance Association, thought that tasting Dog's Nose twice a week for twenty years had lost him the use of his right hand. *Dog's nose, which your committee find upon inquiry to be compounded of warm porter, moist sugar, gin, and nutmeg (a groan, and "So it is!" from an elderly female).*

DOGS NOSE   1 pint Guinness
                             2 oz Gin
                             1 tablespoon brown sugar
                             pinch nutmeg
Put the sugar into the warmed Guinness with the gin and sprinkle nutmeg on top.
Drink it hot.

In the lower windows of the Magpie and Stump in Clare market, *a large black board, announcing in white letters to an enlightened public that there were 500,000 barrels of double stout in the cellars of the establishment, left the mind in a state of not unpleasing doubt and uncertainty as to the precise direction in the bowels of the earth, in which this mighty cavern might be supposed to extend.* One's mind boggles!

It was darkly rumoured that the butler had sometimes mingled porter with Paul's table-beer to make him strong.

SHANDYGAFF   *3 lumps ice*
                         1 liqueur glass Orange brandy
                         juice of half a lemon
                         ½ pint best ale
                         ½ pint ginger beer

Into your favourite tankard put the ice, orange brandy and lemon juice.
Add the best ale and ginger beer and drink with a twist of lemon peel
atop.

Porter to me means Guinness and my memories go back to the time
when pubs in Ireland received their Guinness in barrels. To pour it
out of the wood to appreciative Irishmen? Certainly not. It was so
that the landlord could pour it into bottles and put real corks into
them – what fun to pull them out again! This habit has been
stopped, the more the luck for me because I managed to acquire an
old corking machine – an incredible contraption and a genuine
antique. As such it couldn't be exported from Ireland, but
somehow managed to find its way north in blustery weather, with
rain pouring out of the heavens – on a day when no self-respecting
customs man could be expected to come out of his office. From
there to a factory making office machinery and thence by container
ship to England. I have it yet: it weighs a ton. I only wish I had had
it when I imported a barrel of wine from France.
The Guinness and oyster festival in Galway was a lost week-end. It is
one that will haunt forever. The story of my opening the bedroom
door to our hostess in my altogether reached the banquet before we
did, and when we did, she professed not to recognise me in my
clothes. But oysters, small and succulent and creamy Guinness
really do go well together – made for each other. And yet in the
days under review, oysters were the food of the very poor: *"the
poorer a place is,"* said Sam, *"the greater call there seems to be for
oysters. Look here, sir; here's a oyster stall to every half-dozen
houses. The street's lined vith 'em. Blessed if I don't think that ven a
man's wery poor, he rushes out of his lodgings, and eats oysters in
reg'lar desperation."* *"To be sure he does,"* said Mr Weller senior;
"and its just the same vith pickled salmon!"
To me Guinness should be drunk in Ireland in its natural state

– unadulterated, even by champagne.

    BLACK VELVET   *½ pint champagne*
                                    ½ pint Guinness
Into a pint silver tankard pour the champagne, and carefully on top
the Guinness.

"Did you ever taste beer?"
"I had sip of it once," said the small servant.
"Here's a state of things!" cried Mr Swivvler, "She NEVER tasted it
– it can't be tasted in a sip."

BRANDY

So, to keep up their good humour, they stopped at the first roadside
tavern they came to, and ordered a glass of brandy and water all
round, with a magnum of extra strength for Mr Samuel Weller.
Brandy was the gentleman's drink. It bore a high duty and was
expensive. The most desirable came, as it does today, from Cognac;
but there were other sources and some clever imitations. In A Tale
of Two Cities, Cly compliments Madame Defarge, *"Marvellous*
Cognac!" It was the first time it had ever been so complimented,
and Madame Defarge knew enough about its antecedents to know
better. She said, however, that the cognac was flattered, and took
up her knitting.
Brandy is mentioned forty-four times in Pickwick Papers, and
Mr Pickwick himself called it exhilarating. He also had recourse to
it in times of stress, as when released from the pound in Bury.
Again, when Dodson and Fogg had been playing battledore and
shuttlecock with him, he was rather ruffled. He wanted a glass of
brandy and water warm: *"Where can I have it, Sam?"* Mr Weller's
knowledge of London was extensive and peculiar and he directed

Marvellous Cognac

him without the slightest consideration to a nearby public house which had a table without a leg in the middle, *"wich all the others has, and its wery inconwenient."*

In a more relaxed mood, at the Great White Horse in Ipswich, Mr Pickwick had finished a miserable supper with Mr Peter Magnus and they *ordered a bottle of the worst possible port wine, at the highest possible price, for the good of the house, drank brandy and water for their own. Mr Peter Magnus was naturally of a very communicative disposition and the brandy and water operated with wonderful effect in warming into life the deepest hidden secrets of his bosom.* (Wimmel effects me in the same way.)

At Dingley Dell, *long after the ladies had retired, did the hot elder wine, well qualified with brandy and spice, go round, and round,*

The Wellers in the Blue Boar

and round again; and sound was the sleep and pleasant were the dreams that followed.

Brandy – a gentleman's drink certainly; yet Sam, earning only £12 a year went into a public house in the City and ordered *nine penn'orth o' brandy and water luke, and the inkstand,* and sat down to write his Valentine. But then Sam *"worn't always a boots, sir. I wos a carrier's boy at startin': then a vagginer's, then a helper, then a boots. Now I'm a gen'l'm'n's servant. I shall be a gen'l'm'n myself one of these days, perhaps, with a pipe in my mouth, and a summer-house in the back garden. Who knows? I shouldn't be surprised, for one."*

Like other spirits brandy was strong and probably rough. Even Mr Samuel Weller was shocked when he reported to Mr Pickwick early on Christmas morning 1827 that *"a couple o' Sawbones – not reg'lar thoroughbred Sawbones – they're only in training – were smokin' cigars by the kitchen fire, and one on 'em's got his legs on the table, and is drinkin' brandy NEAT, vile the tother one – him in the barnacles – has got a barrel o' oysters atween his knees, wich he's a openin' like steam, and as fast as he eats 'em, he takes a aim vith the shells at young dropsy, who's a sittin' down fast asleeep in the chimbley corner."*

Nancy too liked brandy and water, probably because of her profession; but she also drank geneva. And Mrs Petowker, about to be married, made use of the medical properties of brandy.

Mrs Varden wept, and laughed, and sobbed, and shivered, and hiccoughed, and choked; and was supported upstairs by Miss Miggs who administered *warm brandy-and-water not over weak, and divers other cordials, also of a stimulating quality, administered at first in teaspoons and afterwards in increasing doses, and of which Miss Miggs herself partook as a preventative measure (for fainting is infectious).*

One of my early recollections is of my French grandmother, Mumsey, giving me "un canard" – a lump of sugar soaked in brandy and dipped in black coffee. A superb bon-bon for a good boy. I had to assure her that I had not been "un méchant coco", meant in the nicest possible way I am sure.

When I was older, from the same source, came a Brandy Toddy for a cold. It is still very much a favourite in the family.

BRANDY TODDY	1 teaspoon brown sugar
	1 teaspoon honey
	juice of ½ a lemon
	a large measure of brandy

Put the brown sugar and honey into a warmed tumbler. Add juice of half a lemon. Pour on boiling water and stir. Top up with a large measure of brandy.

"Glasses round, – brandy and water, hot and strong, and sweet, and plenty." Thus the stranger, Mr Alfred Jingle, when he first met the Pickwickians at Golden Cross. His advice for a black eye: *"nothing like raw beef-steak for a bruise, sir; cold lamp-post very good, but lamp-post inconvenient – damned odd standing in the open streeet half-an-hour, with your eye against a lamp-post – eh, – very good – ha! ha!"*

Incidentally, brandy, like port, is passed clockwise round the table, but, unlike port, the cork is replaced between rounds to prevent evaporation.

"Bottle stands – pass it round – way of the sun – through the button-hole – no heeltaps."

BRANDY BASED CORDIALS

ORANGE BRANDY –	8 Seville oranges
Auntie Georgie	4 lemons (good sized ones)
(Mrs Chatfield's recipe.)	3 lb loaf sugar
	1 gallon good brandy

Very thinly peel the oranges and lemons and put this into a jar with the sugar which has been pounded fine. Add the brandy and cover the jar tightly. Stir every third day for three weeks. Then strain and bottle, sealing the corks with wax.

Orange Brandy is fit to drink within a few weeks but is best left for two years to let the full flavour come out.

A delectable concoction from Auntie Georgie's note book. She pinched it from Mrs Chatfield – an excellent woman she must have been. Perhaps she was the wife of the clergyman of Dingley Dell: *a stout blooming old lady, who looked as if she were well skilled, not only in the art and mystery of manufacturing home-made cordials greatly to other people's satisfaction, but of tasting them occasionally very much to her own.* Orange Brandy forms the basis of my shandy and should be used in all recipes that call for an orange liqueur.

CHERRY BRANDY
1 lb ripe, sound Morello cherries
1 lb (or slightly under) castor sugar
1 bottle of brandy

Remove the pips from the cherries, reserving twelve. Put the cherries and the sugar in a jar and secure tightly with a stopper, turning the jar upside down two or three times a day for three days. Add the bottle of brandy and the reserved twelve pips which have been cracked. Continue turning for the next three weeks and then store in a dark place for three months. After this time strain the mixture, bottle, and keep for seven years before drinking.

The cherries are excellent served as a sweet.

A substantial lunch, with the agreeable items of strong-beer and cherry-brandy.

I have been making it for so long that I now only drink it ten years old. And wonderful it is.

"Emma, bring out the cherry-brandy."

CASSIS   *1 lb ripe blackcurrants*
                                  ½ lb castor sugar
                                  1 bottle brandy

Put the blackcurrants and sugar into a jar and secure with a stopper.
Turn them two or three times a day for three days. Add the bottle of
brandy and again add stopper and turn two or three times a day for two
weeks. The jar can then be stored in a dark place for three months. After
this time strain and bottle. Cassis is ready for drinking in six months but
will keep.

A cordial made with black currants and brandy. Canon Kir, an
erstwhile Mayor of Dijon, invented a great summer drink, Kir,
which calls for cassis and a dry white burgundy. It becomes a Kir
suprème if a sparkling burgundy is used.

CIDER

CIDER CUP I   *1 liqueur glass brandy*
                                  1 liqueur glass curacao
                                  (or orange brandy)
                                  1 bottle medium cider
                                  1 bottle soda water
                                  2 inches cucumber peel
                                  a little sugar
                                  1 apple

Cut up the apple into a large jug and cover with the brandy, curacao
and a sprinkling of sugar. Cover and leave for at least half an hour.
Add the cider and cucumber peel, and, at the last moment, the soda
water. Stir and drink cold.

There aren't many references to cider in Dickens, but he did have
some in his cellar. *And in the lower windows* of the Magpie and
Stump *dangled two or three printed cards, bearing reference to
Devonshire cider.*
I remember, many years ago, three of us youngsters buying a sailing

boat in Gravesend and celebrating the fact ashore by drinking cider. We were fine in the pub; but out in the cool air, our legs had an extraordinary tendency to give way under us, whilst we still had reasonably clear heads. The result was to want to lie down and roar with laughter. It seemed right that two of us should fall into the dock trying to climb on board. Oh, a fine evening it was! Next morning the boat was named the "Istanbul Hope" – we were hoping to sail her to Constantinople to find buried treasure. In fact, we sailed her out into the Thames, missed the "Jamaica Producer", a banana boat, by an acid drop (well, steam does give way to sail?) and landed her on the mud at high water springs. I draw a tactful veil over the rest of the story – I still blush.

Auntie Georgie's recipe for Cyder Cup is one of our favourites now that we live in Somerset. I have slightly amended it. It is an excellent drink whilst playing that dastardly game of croquet.

CYDER CUP	*4 or 5 large lumps of sugar*
Auntie Georgie – 1859	*the rind of a lemon*
	ice
	2 wine glasses sherry
	1 wine glass brandy
	1 bottle cyder
	1 bottle soda water

GENEVA, HOLLANDS, SCHIEDAM, DUTCH GIN

So called from the French word for juniper – genièvre. Junipers flourished in Holland and the berries were used when the initial spirit was redistilled. This was called genièvre – geneva – and eventually gin.

Mr Trotter accompanied Mr Weller to the tap, where they were soon occupied in discussing an exhilarating compound, formed by mixing together, in a pewter vessel, certain quantities of British

The Goblin visits Gabriel Grub

Hollands, and the fragrant essence of the clove.
In the 1830s there was a distillery in Maidstone which made excellent geneva, sold all over the country, and which probably found its way to nearby Gads Hill.

I have spent many happy hours in Holland trying to decide whether to drink it Younger (jong) or Older (oud). Even today I am not sure of the answer – certainly it has nothing to do with age. Probably one should drink it young as there are less additives – less suffering the next morning.

"He who de Quipers nightly takes soundly sleeps and fresh awakes" moulded on the side of the bottle has a lot of truth in it; but I prefer Bokma.

It is said that "Dutch Courage" comes from English soldiers in Europe fortifying themselves with geneva.

You may not like the first taste; but give it a chance, it is worth it. Said Quilp to Mr Richard Swiveller: *There is a house by the water-side where they have some of the noblest Schiedam – reputed to be smuggled, but that's between ourselves – that can be got in all the world. The landlord knows me."* Mr Quilp called for a wooden keg full of the vaunted liquor and drew it off into the glasses with the

Mr Quilp in a Smoking Humour

skill of a practiced hand, and mixed it with about a third of water.

"Is it good?" said Quilp, as Richard Swiveller smacked his lips, "is it strong and fiery? Does it make you wink and choke, and your eyes water, and your breath come short – does it?"

"Does it?" cried Dick, throwing away part of the contents of his glass, and filling it up with water. "Why, man, you don't mean to tell me that you drink such fire as this?"

"No!" rejoined Quilp. "Not drink it! Look here. And here. And here again. Not drink it!"

As he spoke, Daniel Quilp drew off and drank three small glassfuls of the raw spirit, and then with a horrible grimace took a great many pulls at his pipe, and swallowing the smoke, discharged it in a heavy cloud from his nose.

Maybe that is why I like it followed by a glass of Dutch beer. Old Wardle related the story of Gabriel Grub who was carried away by the goblins. He told it by the huge fire at Manor Farm, Dingley Dell at Christmastide over a bowl of wassail which he poured out with no stinted hand. Gabriel Grub, unlike most undertakers, *was an ill-conditioned, cross-grained, surly fellow – a morose and lonely man, who consorted with nobody but himself, and an old wicker bottle. A little before twilight, one Christmas Eve, Gabriel shouldered his spade, lighted his lantern, and betook himself towards the old churchyard; for he had got a grave to finish by next morning, and, feeling very low, he thought it might raise his spirits, perhaps, if he went on with his work at once.*

Well, he worked for an hour or so and then sat himself on a flat tombstone and drew forth his wicker bottle containing hollands:

"A coffin at Christmas! A Christmas box. Ho! Ho! Ho!"

And then the goblins gave him a good going over for being so miserable, but mostly for drinking hollands – ALONE. What a splendid lesson! Drinking's made for company. Never drink alone, except medicinally.

JOHN COLLINS *juice of ½ lemon*
1 teaspoon powdered sugar
2 oz dutch gin
soda water
2 dashes Angostura

Shake well the lemon juice, sugar and gin with ice and strain into glass.
Add two more cubes of ice and fill with soda water. Top with two dashes
Angostura.
Decorate with slice of lemon, orange and cherry.
Serve with straws.

GIN

DRY MARTINI *Dry gin*
ice
sensation French vermouth

Into a mixing glass full of ice pour at least a quarter of a bottle of dry gin.
Stir and strain into two large goblets. Add – two puffs from a scent spray
containing French vermouth.
I watched this being mixed by a friend in New York. When I gently
remonstrated, he said: "Gee, Cedric, this one is in your honour; I usually
pass the cork over the glass!"

*Gin-drinking is a great vice in England, but wretchedness and dirt
are a greater; and until you improve the homes of the poor, or
persuade a half-famished wretch not to seek relief in the temporary
oblivion of his own misery, with the pittance which, divided among
his family, would furnish a morsel of bread for each, gin-shops will
increase in number and splendour. If Temperance Societies would
suggest an antidote against hunger, filth, and foul air, or could
establish dispensaries for the gratuitous distribution of bottles of
Lethe-water, gin-palaces would be numbered among the things
that were.*

The growth of gin drinking and temperance movements were

The Gin Shop

complimentary. Remember the Brick Lane Branch of the United Grand Junction Ebenezer Temperance Association? One convert was Thomas Burton, a cats-meat purveyor to the Lord Mayor and Sheriffs, and several members of the Common Council: *"Has a wooden leg; finds a wooden leg expensive, going over the stones; used to wear second-hand wooden legs, and drink a glass of hot gin and water regularly every night – sometimes two (deep sighs). Found the second-hand wooden legs split and rot very quickly; is firmly persuaded that their constitution was undermined by the gin and water (prolonged cheering). Buys new wooden legs now, and drinks nothing but water and weak tea. The new legs last twice as long as the others used to do, and he attributes this solely to his temperate habits" (triumphant cheers).*

There are many references to gin with sugar and other sweeteners and flavourings. In the early period under review, spirits must have been pretty beastly and strong too – probably about 100° proof. However things were improving. An Irishman, Aeneas Coffey, developed a new still which produced much purer spirit at less cost. But the strength was still there. It wasn't until after Dickens' death that the legal minimum of spirits was reduced to 75° proof. It was in fact, usually sold at 80°.

Gin was not a respectable drink: even in a punch it wasn't very popular with the nobs. Bob Cratchit, however, turned up his cuffs and *compounded some hot mixture in a jug with gin and lemons, and stirred it round and round and put it on the hob to simmer.*

And Charles Dickens himself particularly loved the ritual of mixing the evening glass of Gin Punch, which he performed with all the energy and discrimination of Mr Micawber.

Mr Micawber's water had been cut off. *To divert his thoughts from this melancholy subject, I informed Mr Micawber that I relied upon him for a bowl of punch, and led him to the lemons. His recent despondency, not to say despair, was gone in a moment. I never saw a man so thoroughly enjoy himself amid the fragrance of lemon-peel and sugar, the odour of burning spirit, and the steam of boiling water, as Mr Micawber did that afternoon. It was wonderful to see his face shining at us out of a thin cloud of these delicate*

Mr Micawber delivers some Valedictory Remarks

fumes, as he stirred, and mixed, and tasted, and looked as if he were making, instead of a punch, a fortune for his family down to the latest posterity.

GIN PUNCH
Mr Micawber's favourite

Juice ½ lemon
pinch ground cinnamon
1 clove
1 teaspoon brown sugar
1 teaspoon honey
1 large measure sweet dark Madeira
1 large measure dry gin
grated nutmeg

Into a warm tumbler put the juice of half a lemon, the cinnamon and clove, and the sugar and honey. Threequarters fill the glass with boiling water, add the madeira and gin and stir with a stick of cinnamon. Grate nutmeg thereon and drink quickly.

The recipe doesn't sound very exciting, but the product is exquisite.
"And whatever you do, young woman, don't bring more than a
shilling's-worth of gin and water warm when I rings the bell a
second time: for that is always my allowance, and I never takes a
drop beyond!"
In Egypt, during the early 1940's, the armed forces found the diet
of hump of camel distasteful and monotonous. To alleviate the
situation they took "Swissitch":
One Swissitch gives an appetite – even the hump appears inviting;
two or more makes food unnecessary. Salt of course is a must in the
heat.

SWISSITCH   *1 teaspoon salt*
                             1 large tot gin
                             ¼ lemon or lime
Put the salt into your mouth and swirl around with the gin. Swallow, and
at the same time pop the lemon in, biting on it fiercely.

Around 1830 when beer shops were being opened, the consumption
of gin was held at about seven million gallons a year. But by 1845 it
had risen to some nine millions.
Gin was sold from the wood in barrels or from porcelain kegs. It
wasn't until the 1914-18 war that bottles came into their own.
A couple of ladies, who, having imbibed the contents of various
'three-outs' of gin-and-bitters in the course of the morning, have at
length differed on some point, and – in short – went at each other
hammer and tongs. The bitters were almost certainly Angostura.

PINK GIN   ,   *Dash Angostura bitters*
                             1 large tot Plymouth gin
                             (or any dry London gin)
Roll about six drops of Angostura around a wine glass and pour in the
gin. Add an equal quantity of iced water or more to taste.

BURNT PINK GIN   *1 teaspoon Angostura*
                                1 large tot dry gin
Pour the gin into a wine glass and burn the Angostura in a teaspoon by
heating over flame. When well burning let it fall into the gin. Add cold
water to taste.

Mrs Gamp, with the bottle on one knee, and the glass on the other,
sat upon a stool, shaking her head for a long time, until, in a
moment of abstraction, she poured out a dram of spirits, and raised
it to her lips. It was succeeded by a second, and by a third –."
Mrs Gamp's *spirits, from motives of delicacy, she kept in a tea-pot.*
"Mrs Harris," I says, "leave the bottle on the chimley-piece, and
don't ask me to take none, but let me put my lips to it when I am so
dispoged."

GIN BASED CORDIALS

SLOE GIN   *1 lb ripe, sound, plump sloes*
                                1 lb castor sugar
                                1 bottle dry gin
Prick the sloes with a silver fork all over. Put them and the sugar in a jar
and cover tightly with screw stopper to exclude air. Turn two or three
times daily for three days, and then add the gin. Restopper and continue
turning until the sugar is quite dissolved. Store in dark place for three
months. Now strain and bottle. Cork well and keep for seven years.

Sloes are the fruit of the blackthorn. They are small, dark purple,
hard and very sour berries. The traditional stirrup cup was drunk
with Sloe Gin, one of the nicest liqueurs for those who don't like
sticky sweet drinks.
The recipe is old and simple. As with other such drinks, the fruit

and sugar are combined for two or three days and turned periodically. The spirit is then added and the turning process continued until the sugar has completely disappeared. I find that the lavatory is the perfect place to keep the jars during this period: anyone using it must turn the jar.

DAMSON GIN   *As for Sloe Gin*
                               but substitute damsons
The damsons, when strained off, like the cherries, are excellent to eat.
They should be reserved for cups and other drinks calling for fruit.

With all home-made liqueurs it is essential to lay down a large stock in the early years. Try to keep them for seven years before drinking. I don't know whether the liquor improves with the passing years; but to be able to say, honestly, when allowing a friend to taste, that it is thus and thus age is extremely rewarding.

MADEIRA

Sol Gills *lighted a candle, and went down below into a little cellar, while his nephew, standing on the mouldy staircase, dutifully held the light. After a moment's groping here and there, he presently returned with a very ancient-looking bottle, covered with dust and dirt.*
"Why, Uncle Sol!" said the boy, "what are you about? That's the wonderful madeira! - there's only one more bottle!"
References to madeira are numerous, especially to old, rare and wonderful madeira. Even the ordinary wine appears many times; Mr Weller emerged *from a sequestered spot, where he had been engaged in discussing a bottle of Madeira, which he had abstracted*

Bleak House

from the breakfast-table, an hour or two before. "Here's your servant, sir. Proud o' the title, as the Living Skellington said, ven they show'd him."

My earliest recollections of madeira are of Sunday mornings in the summer. Guests of my parents were required to remove six weeds from the tennis lawn and to fill the holes with a mixture of compost and grass seed. Only then were they allowed a glass of madeira and a slice of cake – or was it a slice of madeira and a glass of marsala? It became almost impossible to earn that glass as the season progressed. I suspect that I took pity on them and "borrowed" some weeds from a neighbour – for a consideration, no doubt.

Charles Dickens was a great friend of the Watsons of Rockingham Castle. In fact, much of the castle is described in Bleak House. I am delighted that Commander Michael Saunders-Watson still lives there. I am even happier to have his permission to copy Charles' letter to his great-grandmother, in which he sent her his recipe for "Moonbeams". Visit the castle near Market Harborough to see the letter and re-live some of the Bleak House episodes.

MOONBEAMS FOR SUMMER DRINKING

Pour into a jug in this proportion:
10 wine glasses of Madeira
⅔ wine glass brandy
4 wine glasses water

Add peel of a small lemon cut very thin. Sweeten to taste. Plunge into the whole a brown toast. Grate a little nutmeg over the surface. Tie a cloth over the jug and stand in a cool place or in cold water until needed.

In 1846 Charles Dickens sent this recipe to Mrs Watson of Rockingham Castle.

"There is no better way for a man to find out whether he is really asleep or awake, than calling for something to eat. If he's in a dream, gentlemen, he'll find something wanting in the flavour, depend upon it.

Tom explained his doubts to the old gentleman, and said that if there was any cold meat in the house, it would ease his mind very much to test himself at once. The old gentleman ordered up a

venison pie, a small ham, and a bottle of very old madeira. At the
first mouthful of the pie and the first glass of wine, Tom smacks his
lips and cries out, "I'm awake – wide awake;" and to prove that he
was so, gentlemen, he made an end of 'em both."

PORT

Mr Tulkinghorn *has a priceless binn of port in some artful cellar*
under the Fields, which is one of his many secrets. When he dines
alone in chambers, he descends with a candle to the echoing regions
below the deserted mansion, and, heralded by a remote reverbera-
tion of thundering doors, comes gravely back, encircled by an
earthy atmosphere, and carrying a bottle from which he pours a
radiant nectar, two score and ten years old, that blushes in the glass
to find itself so famous, and fills the whole room with the fragrance
of southern grapes.
I disagree with his philosophy of drinking good port alone. I understand it; but port is a wine to be shared and discussed.
In the 17th and early 18th centuries, port was a Burgundy type
wine, harsh, dry and heady; a wine to satisfy the cold, carnivorous
English squire, fortified ever since the head of a noble firm of wine
growers in the Douro once poured several gallons of brandy into a
cask to stop it refermenting.
Boswell said of it: "a bottle of thick English port is a very heavy and
very inflamatory dose. I felt it last time that I drank it for several
days, and this morning it was boiling in my veins."
It wasn't until the mid-18th century that an unknown cellarman
introduced the brandy at an early stage of the original ferment, and
produced port as we know it today – probably by mistake.
Let us consider the various types of port. Vintage port may be
defined broadly as a wine made exclusively from grapes of one

exceptional year which must be declared by the grower. It is usually bottled about the second year, and allowed to mature slowly for twelve to twenty years, or more.

A Late Bottled Port is made from grapes of a single year. It is kept in cask for from three to six years before bottling. Port matures more quickly in wood.

A Crusting or Crusted Port is a blend of two or three different years bottled after three to four years. It is a high quality wine.

Tawny Port is also a blend of several years, but is matured in cask for anything up to forty years or more The longer it matures in wood, the lighter it becomes. Some people prize an old tawny even more than a vintage port – certainly my grandfather did: "There is no vice in a wood port."

Finally, Ruby Port is a younger wine and is, according to Raymond Postgate, "the basic sound ordinaire of the port world."

Mr Tupman applied himself with great interest to the port wine.

In Pickwick Papers, Mr Boffer, a stockbroker, had some fine 1764 port in his cellar. This simple statement has caused port experts to rush into print. How can this be? The first great vintage year was 1775. 1764 is therefore out of the question – bunkum. And yet nobody knows when the first vintage was declared.

This had led to "The Great Port Controversy" (see Appendix 1), a conflict of opinion which should have been as acrimonious as Mr Pickwick's *Theory of Tittlebats;* however, the very gentle gentlemen who understand this sublime wine cannot be acrimonious.

Nevertheless, it lead to a meeting of many of the world's greatest port pundits. Over luncheon in the cellars of John Davy, Free Vintner, "The Great Port Controversy" was debated. After several hours serious speculation, it was agreed unanimously that another lunch would be necessary if any light at all was to be shed on this very important subject.

Port was the Englishman's drink, drunk in the early days, even in India, which probably accounted for generals dying at the ripe old age of thirty.

Mr Pickwick had dined, finished his second pint of particular port, pulled his silk handkerchief over his head, put his feet on the

Mr F's Aunt is Conducted into Retirement

fender, and thrown himelf back in an easy-chair, when the entrance of Mr Weller with his carpet-bag aroused him from his tranquil meditations.

The quantity of port in the Gads Hill cellar indicates that Dickens served port whenever he entertained. Certainly my grandfather did.

On becoming an assize judge, he decided that members of the bar should have a good time. Instead of inviting the bar en bloc to one large dinner during the circuit, he held several cosy little parties at different towns. With this in mind, he laid in a stock of first-rate champagne and fine old port. On one occasion, my father Pip acted as his Marshal. He was entirely responsible for seeing that the wines were sent on in advance to assure their perfect condition for the dinners. Pip was a great judge of port – one of the best; but then, what an upbringing! Few of us today have a chance to know port as he knew it.

Once, for Pip's birthday, I consulted Keith Stevens of the old City wine firm, Corney & Barrow: what could I set before Pip to baffle him? Keith was sceptical. After due consideration he discarded the two great years, 1908 and 1912, and suggested one of the few ports shipped in 1911. I decanted the wine with great care and ceremoniously placed it before my father with birthday wishes, inviting him to tell us all about it.

"Well (sniff – sniff –), it isn't the '12; nor the '08." He contemplated the colour and viscosity and had another profound smell. "Was any shipped in between? Why, yes, of course, Offley did in '10; but then (sniff, sniff), it isn't Offley." Keith hadn't told me about that one! "No, it must an '11." We held our breath. He took another smell, rolled the wine around the glass appreciatively and tasted it – smiled – and pronounced it, rightly, Sandeman '11. Furthermore, he told us that Martinez and Rebello Valente had also shipped that year.

Mr Pickwick *had gradually passed through the various stages which precede the lethargy produced by dinner, and its consequences. He had undergone the ordinary transitions from the height of conviviality to the depth of misery, and from the depth of misery to the height of conviviality. Like a gas lamp in the street, with the wind in the pipe, he had exhibited for a moment an unnatural brilliancy; then sunk so low as to be scarcely discernable; after a short interval he had burst out again, to enlighten for a moment, then flickered with an uncertain, staggering sort of light, and then gone out altogether."*

In the old days, a father would lay down a pipe of port for his eldest son. Not a bottle was to be touched until his 21st birthday. An amiable tradition. Pip did manage to put a case of Sandeman '17 down for me; great, except that when I was eighteen, there was only one bottle left and we drank it together.

Which reminds me of the time Pip gave me lunch at the old Conservative Club in St James Street. Ted Sandeman was there and insisted on being introduced to the son of his old friend. He pottered off and produced a bottle of 1887 Jubilee port from his own cellar in the club for my especial edification.

In 1959, when my father-in-law Colonel Arthur ffrench Blake was 80, I managed to acquire another bottle of Jubilee port from John Davy. The price, I remember well, was only eight pounds ten shillings, and Dad sold the empty bottle with its lovely glass medallion for ten pounds. Bless him.

"Bottle stands – pass it round – way of the sun – through the button hole – no hell taps." The button hole is on the left lapel, the way port is customarily passed round the table – passed without the stopper. As soon as it is replaced, your host has indicated clearly that you've had enough.

Pupsey drank his share of vintage port, but later in life he advised: "Whiskers," (I was born bright red with black hair all over), "Whiskers, stick to wood port." It is kept long in cask and is undoubtedly kinder to the liver. At home he always drank Berry Bros wood port. Vintage port gave him "crinkly toes" at night, wood port never did. If you love vintage port at night, make sure to drink a pint of Angostura and soda before retiring.

Port was the base for a number of drinks: *"we will discuss your affairs this very afternoon, over a Christmas bowl of smoking bishop."* Bishop seems to have been a very popular drink, and no wonder. I discovered it many years ago and it quickly became a traditional winter party drink. Not only is its taste exquisite, but equally its medicinal qualities are great. You can feel it doing good. Temperatures go up, from the top of the head (bald heads turn red) right down to the toes.

SMOKING BISHOP   *6 seville oranges* o. 5 Sweet oranges + 1 grapefruit
                                    ¼ lb sugar
                                    1 bottle Portuguese red wine 2 bots cheap strong red
                                    1 bottle port
                                    cloves

Bake the oranges in the oven until they are pale brown, and then put
them into a warmed eathenware bowl with five cloves pricked into each.
Add the sugar and pour in the wine - not the port. Cover and leave in a
warm place for about a day.
Squeeze the oranges into the wine and pour it through a sieve. Add the
port and heat, but do not boil. Serve in warmed goblets and drink hot.
Seville oranges are imported into England only in January and February.
But make this grand medicinal drink in large quantities then and you
will have Bishop's Cup available in the summer and Smoking Bishop for
Christmas. To do this don't add the port, but fortify it with a tot of
Orange Brandy.
Before serving add the port and half pint of water.

*Mr Feeder, after imbibing several custard-cups of negus, began to
enjoy himself.*
Even Negus, a watered down form of Bishop, is good. Mr Stiggins
of pineapple rum propensity, *recommended a bottle of port wine,
warmed with a little water, spice and sugar, as being grateful to the
stomach, and savouring less of the vanity than many other
compounds.*
*No supper did Miss Potterson take that night, and only half her
usual tumbler of hot Port Negus.*

NEGUS   *2 oz lump sugar*
                                    2 lemons
                                    1 bottle port
                                    1 pint boiling water
                                    grated nutmeg

Rub the lumps of sugar on the rinds of the lemons until yellow. Put into a
large warm bowl, adding the strained juice of the lemons. Pour in the
port and add the boiling water when ready to serve, with grated nutmeg
atop. Add more sugar to taste.

RUM

"I am afraid, Samuel, that his feelings have made him athirst indeed."
So said Mrs Weller, mournfully.
"Wot's your usual tap, Sir?" replied Sam.
"Oh my dear young friend," replied Mr Stiggins, "all taps is vanities!"
"Well," said Sam, "I des-say they may be, sir; but which is your partickler wanity. Vich wanity do you like the flavour on best, sir?"
"Oh, my dear young friend, I despise them all. If," said Mr Stiggins, "if there is any one of them less odious than another, it is the liquor called rum. Warm, my dear young friend, with three lumps of sugar to the tumbler."
"Wery sorry to say, sir", said Sam, "that they don't allow that partickler wanity to be sold in this here establishment."
"Oh, the hardness of heart of these inveterate men! ejaculated Mr Stiggins. "Oh, the accursed cruelty of these inhuman persecutors!"
So he had to make do with Negus.

Rum was roughly classified with gin – a spirit for the common folk, moving into the upper classes only as punch. It is odd that there was none in the cellar at Gads Hill. To be sure Dickens died in June, and rum was a winter drink; however the sale catalogued five dozen Pine Apple Rum.

> *PINE APPLE RUM*   *1 pineapple*
> *1 bottle dark rum*
> *sugar*
> Slice a pineapple very thinly, sprinkle with a little sugar and leave for a
> day. Set aside two slices and press the juice out of the rest adding to it an
> equal amount of sweetened rum (two oz sugar to half a pint rum). Put
> into a jar with the spare slices of pineapple. Leave, well stoppered, for
> three weeks. Strain and bottle.

But it goes to show that the rascally deputy shepherd of the Dorking Branch of the United Grand Junction Ebenezer Temperance

The Red-nosed man Discourseth

Association had good taste – both his wanities are worth drinking, Pine Apple Rum and Negus:

Mr Stiggins took down a tumbler, and with great deliberation put four lumps of sugar in it. Then with the tumbler half-full of pineapple rum, advanced to the kettle which was singing gaily on the hob, mixed his grog, stirred it, sipped it, sat down, and taking a long and hearty pull at the rum and water, stopped for breath. He visited the Marquis of Granby very often and took with him a *"flat bottle as holds about a pint and a half, and fills it vith the pineapple rum afore he goes avay."*

On the 1931 trip, I relaxed at the end of the Aquatic Club pier in Barbados sipping Green Swizzles, surrounded by clear crystal water and brilliantly white coral sand, seemingly just under the water, but in fact some twenty feet down – what a paradise! I hope this little book is a success; I would like to go back to the land of the Swizzles to relax over a real Green Swizzle in its native surroundings. I understand sadly there are few remaining masters of the art of mixing a Green Swizzle.

Two years later in Kingston, Jamaica, I was lucky enough to be given a rum that was a hundred years old. It was white and incredibly smooth: but then, so was a potheen I once drank in Ireland, and that was about the same age. Potheen is an illicit Irish spirit: It is normally rough and fiery and, if given to cattle, cures coughs. Quilp would have appreciated it.

Mrs Sparsit had a violent cold which Mr Bounderby tried to cure with *potent restoratives, such as screwing the patient's thumbs, smiting her hands, abundently watering her face, and inserting salt in her mouth.* When these failed he angrily packed her home in a coach to the Bank with the advice that she should *"put your feet into the hottest water you can bear, and take a glass of scalding rum-and-butter after you get into bed".*

Also whilst in Jamaica, I was taken on a fishing trip in the north of the island. Apart from wading across the mouth of a river at midday to find a good picnic place, and shooting alligators from the same spot that night, my memory is of being woken up in the morning with a Rum Punch and listening to the midday news from

HOT BOWL PUNCH
John Greaves

2 measures rum
1 measure sweet vermouth
1 measure orange juice
peppercorns ⎤
cinnamon ⎥
root ginger ⎬ to taste
cloves ⎦

Simmer the orange juice and spices for half an hour. Add rum and vermouth and pour into warmed glasses to which half a teaspoon of sugar has been added.

London. In those days all twelve of Big Ben's chimes were broadcast. It was called the golden minute and was listened to in silence. On the last day of our visit I was taken round a rummery in the cool of the morning. Later I just managed to climb on board ship as the gangway was being removed - at four o'clock in the afternoon. It was the only time I have ever seen double and I still remember the difficulty of testing the quality of that duality of seagulls flying round the boat. It is a recurring nightmare.

"My dear, Mrs Gamp can drink a glass of rum."

A glorious red-headed cousin bought me a pint of Angostura and soda. Too late to save the day, but it certainly proved its worth. I awoke at four o'clock next morning for a swim in the ship's pool, feeling as fit as a fiddle. The only serious effect was a deep-rooted antipathy to rum - and then I joined the Navy with its "Free Issue."

Mrs Jellyby has been disappointed in Borrioboola-Gha, which turned out a failure in consequence of the king of Borrioboola wanting to sell everybody - who survived the climate - for Rum.

Unpleasant things tend to be forgotten: I can now enjoy rum. Try it on a blustery day while sailing - equal quantities of rum and condensed milk in a tablespoon.

SHERRY

"What thall it be, Thquire, while you wait? thall it be therry? Give it a name, Thquire."
A popular drink of the day, as the cellar shows. *The old lady insists on your swallowing two glasses of sherry before your exert yourself talking.*
And having swallowed them I am reminded immediately of 1940 when I tried to evacuate the Govenor of Guernsey. He had already gone, but the Bailiff insisted on my sharing a pint of sherry with him out of pewter pots from Trinity Hall - our old college. He, poor fellow, had to stay on the island awaiting occupation.
Mr Bucket frequently observes that he likes a toothful of your fine old brown East Inder sherry better than anything you can offer him. Consequently he fills and empties his glass, with a smack of his lips.
Later I was lucky enough to visit Gibraltar and even luckier to know the Chief of Police. He gave me an introduction to his splendid old Spanish wine merchant. In his cellars I asked for a dry sherry with a lot of body to it! By the third and last day, I - we (I now had with me, the Captain, Number One, Doc and Chiefy) had tasted some hundred or so sherries and eventually bought La Ina in vast quantities. It was in fact the first wine he had given me to taste; but what a party! The midshipman had cleverly been kept on board throughout our stay and it was he who piloted us out of harbour on a night as dark as the inside of a cow.
"But come, this is dry work. Let's rinse our mouths with a drop of burnt sherry."
Sherry Cobbler is a delectable summer drink and looks most appealing - a long frosted glass with a slice of orange on top and port filtering through gives the whole a thrilling and inviting appearance.

SHERRY COBBLER   *1 measure fresh orange juice*
                         a little sugar
                         1 measure medium sherry
                         1 tablespoon port
                         ice
                         slice of orange

Put sugar into a tumbler with crushed ice. Add the orange juice and
sherry and stir. Place on top the slice of orange with two straws through
the middle. Pour the port on top of the orange.

But on its own, one glass of sherry suffices – it does my liver no
good.

*When the time drew near for retiring, Mr Bounderby took a glass of
water. "Oh, Sir!" said Mrs Sparsit. "Not your sherry warm, with
lemon-peel and nutmeg?" "Why, I have got out of the habit of
taking it now, ma'am," said Mr Bounderby. "The more's the pity,
Sir," returned Mrs Sparsit; "you are losing all your good old habits."*

One of my great-grandfather's favourite lunch drinks was sherry
and seltzer; when exhausted by public readings, he used to have an
egg beaten up in sherry during the interval.

Mr Chillip had *a glass of warm Sherry Negus at his elbow.*

SHERRY NEGUS   *3 oz lump sugar*
                        2 lemons
                        1 bottle sherry
                        1 pint boiling water
                        grated nutmeg

Rub the lumps of sugar on the rinds of the lemons until yellow.
Put into large warm bowl adding the strained juice of the lemons.
Pour in the sherry and add the boiling water when ready to serve.
Grate nutmeg on top.

WHISKEY

Whiskies with an "e" come from countries other than Scotland.
There is an excellent malt from Ireland, and bourbon has its place.
To be sure, there was one which claimed to be a de luxe, double
distilled, patent bourbon. I bought it in Australia to create for my
hosts a delectable Bourbon Sour – in every way the right tipple to
repay their kindness. It should have been a drink fit for the gods,
but I know I poured mine down the sink. The bottle still remains in
their drink cupboard – no one even has the courage to touch it.
Nevertheless, I maintain that a Bourbon Sour, properly made with
the right bourbon, is delicious. I always have one when visiting the
bar of the Stafford Hotel in London to see my old friends, Louis and
Charles. It is a drink to sustain and give confidence – something a
country bumpkin needs when visiting London these days.
Perhaps, too, bourbon is nostalgic. It takes me back to a wonderful
weekend in New Orleans when I was honoured to visit that earliest
of Pickwick Clubs which was founded in 1857. There I drank a
stupendous jorum of Mint Julep. It was so good that I now make
one every year at home. As soon as the mint is in perfect condition,
I put the necessaries into the freezer and invite a strong and
appreciative friend for the following day. It is a ceremony that must
be prepared in every detail, but it is worth it: and remember that
one bottle of bourbon is just right for two.

BOURBON SOUR   *juice of ½ lemon*
                      1 teaspoon powdered sugar
                      2 dashes Angostura
                      2 oz Bourbon
                      ice
Shake all the ingredients with the ice and strain into glass allowing a little
ice to fall into glass. Decorate with half a slice of lemon and a cherry.

Whilst in New Orleans I was also a guest of the Boston Club and

given a glass of their impeccable punch. I have permission to reproduce the recipe here.

BOSTON CLUB PUNCH   1 oz water
(New Orleans)   1 bar-spoon sugar
                          juice of ½ a lemon
                          4 or 5 dashes of orange flower water
                          2 jiggers bourbon whiskey

Put the ingredients into a shaker with lumped ice and shake well. Pour into a chilled old-fashioned glass. Add two bar-spoons of cherry juice, one cherry and a slice of lemon and serve.

WHISKY

Although brandy was the popular drink, it is fascinating to find Dickens mentioning whisky many times during the first two years of his writing. After that it hardly appears at all. In the first of the short stories, collected into Sketches by Boz, he spelt it whisky, as we do today when referring to scotch. A few months later he was spelling it whiskey with an "e" – this may have followed popular English spelling. As late as 1909 a Royal Commission of Inquiry into Whiskey and other Potable Spirits used the "e".

Charles' knowledge of whisky must have come from his future father-in-law, George Hogarth, who was then music correspondent on The Morning Chronicle. Hogarth hailed from Edinburgh and certainly drank whisky. Dickens himself visited Edinburgh for the paper in 1834 and perhaps "The Bagman's Uncle" was founded on fact.

Only a small amount of whisky was imported into London. The Morning Advertiser and The Morning Post mentioned it. In the sketch "Making a Night of it", after dinner our two heroes partake of two goes of the best scotch whisky and warm water and sugar – so

Doughty Street
Monday Evening

My Dear Sir

It will give Mrs. Dickens much
pleasure to see the ladies of your
family on Wednesday, — and both
she and I will be most happy
to dine with you on the 29th.

Accept my best thanks for
the Highland Whiskey, which,
as in honor bound, I intend
trying this very night. As I shall
be at work on Nickleby, you will
know what has inspired me, if
the next number should contain
anything specially good

My Dear Sir, I am,
Very truly Yours
CHARLES DICKENS

John Noble Esquire

Letter to John Noble – 21 January, 1839

they went on, talking politics, puffing cigars, and sipping whisky-and-water. After certain other goes they move on to the theatre where one falls fast asleep – *such were the happy effects of Scotch whisky and Havannahs.*

And "Our Next Door Neighbour" *displayed a most extraordinary partiality for sitting up till three or four o'clock in the morning, drinking whiskey-and-water, and smoking cigars.*

In Pickwick, the old man at the Magpie and Stump tells the story of the poor man *who took an old, damp, rotten set of chambers, in one of the most ancient Inns. Sitting down before the fire at night, drinking the first glass of two gallons of whisky he had ordered on credit,* he saw a ghost and got rid of it by the simple process of suggesting that it would do better to haunt a fairer place than those moth-eaten old chambers in the disagreeable climate of London.

My knowledge of whisky dates from a 1945-48 stint in India. But during the war, whilst serving in HMS Philante (Tommy Sopwith's beautiful yacht), a good background had been laid. Sopwith's old crew, mostly from the Outer Hebrides, saw to that, especially when we were based at Rothesay and Tobermorey. My birthday coincided with the Rothesay visit and I was introducd to Duke's Nose – a large tot of whisky chased by a pint of strong ale. I didn't last long, but long enough to notice that all the pubs were run by cousins of either the old Captain or Mate. In Tobermorey too, the Mishnish Hotel was run by the first cousin of the one, and the Chief of Police (the only policemen on the island) was the first cousin of the other. When we visited at night, the locals were cleared out, the policemen went home, put his cloth cap on and then joined us. I was sorry for the locals until I found them drinking happily in another part of the house.

There were two fine distilleries in Tobermorey. I thought I had found the world's most glorious liquor, and took a bottle to whisky-starved Pip in London, instructing him to forgo his soda and drink it with plain water. It was quite horrible by comparison. It was then that I learnt that the water is so important – it must be soft. The burn, tumbling down from the hills, through the main street and into the harbour, was as brown as the whisky itself – and it was a dark one. On my next visit home, I took one bottle of whisky and two of the local water. How popular I was!

A friend of mine was chairman of a little company producing Antiquary, a grand liqueur whisky. One of the founders, a Mr Hardie, had a very Victorian wife who decided he was drinking too much whisky. Being canny, he said not a word, but arranged that Antiquary, which was then a typically dark whisky, would in future become very light. He drank as much as he had done heretofore, maybe a little more; she thought he was qualifying it well, and they lived happily together for many more years.

ATHOLBROSE   1 teaspoon liquid honey
                              1 tablespoon cream
                              double tot finest liqueur whisky
                              ice
Shake all the ingredients and pour into a favourite glass.
A recipe given me by a good Scot. He didn't think I would enjoy
"porridge".

I remember learning a similar lesson when very young in my grand-parents' home. Mumsey would bustle in and out of the dining room after breakfast, when Pupsey was drinking his last cup of coffee and reading The Times. She would give him his instructions for the day, enquiring about such important matters as to whether he had got the right pants and vest on! I can see him now: "Yes Marie - no Marie - no Marie." Young as I was, I knew he never heard a word and was answering, correctly as it happened, from the tone of her voice. Incidentally, in those days, Mumsey ironed every sheet of The Times so that the printers ink shouldn't come off on his hands.

I learnt another good lesson from my Antiquary friend: never to buy whisky in a fancy bottle, unless of course for a collection. In those days Antiquary was sold in simple and unadorned amber bottles with a discreet label. His message was simple - why pay for the glass?

In India I learnt that whisky is drunk medicinally. I thought, gin drinker that I had been through 1939-45, that this advice was given tongue in cheek; but, my goodness, never was better advice given. In the evening, a gentle walk from the Bombay office to the Yacht Club for a chota-peg in a tumbler of soda water was a wonderful pick-me-up after the tiring heat of the day. One only, back to the flat to bathe, and to dress slowly under the punkah (there was no air-conditioning) with a long gin and tonic, Tom Collins or Gin Sour in hand. Medicinal whisky had to be a blend – Queen Anne was the tipple although George IV was popular if obtainable. Malt was practically unknown, but in evidence after dinner on special occasions.

I once discovered a bottle of "Charles Dickens" whisky in a small shop in a township north of Sydney. I had the label until recently. I am told that there is no such thing as bad scotch. Charles Dickens whisky is no longer produced.

Until 1940 Pip drank a virgin grain, but it is an acquired taste. The Gads Hill cellar boasted a Very Fine Old Highland Whiskey from Cockburn and Company of Leith. They still produce it and I have a bottle in my "cellar".

Whisky perhaps, like champagne, should be drunk on its own. Nevertheless, there are mixed drinks which merit inclusion for medicinal purposes. Probably the most important is Long Life. Kept in small bottles and carried in the pocket or hand-bag, it is a vital piece of equipment for everyday modern life. It is amazing how many emergencies there are in a day, and wonderful to see how quickly they disappear under this treatment.

LONG LIFE   *12 eggs*
                         12 lemons
                         1 pint cream
                         1 bottle liqueur whisky

Carefully wash and dry the eggs. Put into earthenware bowl with the juice of twelve lemons. Cover and leave for five to six days or until the shells are completely dissolved. Whisk well and add cream and whisky. Pour into small bottles suitable for carrying in pocket or hand-bag.

WINE

CEREMONY OF THE LOVING CUP
An ancient feature of City Livery Company Feasts. The Cup is of silver or
silver gilt and filled with spiced wine, immemorially called Sack.
Some Companies prefer plain champagne. Immediately after the dinner
and grace, the Master and Wardens drink a hearty welcome to their
visitors; the Cup is then passed round the table going to the left where
possible. The procedure is for the person who pledges with the Loving
Cup to stand and bow to his neighbour who, also standing, removes the
cover with his right hand and holds it while the other drinks. At the same
time the neighbour on the right of the person pledging stands behind him
while he drinks. The custom giving rise to these actions is said to have
originated in the precaution to keep employed the right, or "dagger",
hand of the person removing the cover, while the person standing behind
the one who is pledging guards his back against any such treachery – such
as that practiced by Elfrida on the unsuspecting King Edward the Martyr
at Corfe Castle, who was slain while drinking.
Traditions vary slightly with the Companies.

Mrs Gamp came into the room, *curtseying to Mrs Mould. At the
same moment a peculiar fragrance was borne upon the breeze, as if
a passing fairy had hiccoughed, and had previously been to a wine
vaults.*

ROSE CUP   *6 well perfumed deep red roses*
                              a little castor sugar
                              1 bottle of white wine
                              1 bottle of sparkling white wine
                              (from the same region)
                              A little borage
Sugar the flower petals of the roses in a jar, pour over them the bottle
of still white wine. It is important to cork this up for six hours or more.
Pour the resultant glorious liquid through a sieve into the container from
which it will be served, pressing the rose petals. Add the borage and the
bottle of *well chilled* sparkling wine just before serving.
The drink is pink with a superb rose bouquet – nectar to sip.

Charles Dickens deals with wine pretty thoroughly – at least his characters drink their fair share. In those days most of it came from Portugal and Spain. The duty on French wine was penal – more than double that on other wines. It was a way of showing our disapproval of the French – a form of economic warfare.

In Dickens' youth, more than half the wine came from Portugal and nearly a quarter from Spain. French wines accounted only for some 5 per cent. In 1860 Gladstone introduced his Free Trade budget, and by the time Dickens died in 1870, Portuguese wines had declined to less than a quarter, Spain had increased to nearly half, and France had secured 20 per cent of the market.

Dickens certainly knew about, and drank, French, German and other wines; but, being the good reporter that he was, refers mostly to the popular drinks of the time: many of the wines mentioned in his works are ports and sherries.

Bishop and Negus demonstrate the popularity of Portuguese wines. They are indeed lovely drinks and appear a number of times. Early in Pickwick Papers, the stranger had fallen foul of Dr Slammer of the 97th Regiment by cutting in on the widow at the ball at the Bull Hotel, Rochester. He was completely unruffled when the furious doctor demanded his card. *"Oh! I see," said the stranger, half aside, "negus too strong here – liberal landlord – very foolish – very – lemonade much better –."* Dr Slammer, seething with wrath, said that he would find him out. *"Rather you found me out than found me at home," replied the unmoved stranger.*

My enjoyment of life is enhanced by drink. I bless my abstemious grandmother for educating me by such artifices as "Un Canard"; the brandy toddy for a cold; and the wine she allowed on high days and holidays – always mixed with water. Because of her my first language was French; but this I quickly and sadly lost at my first English school.

As a direct result of my almost non-existent French, on 15th October 1966 I was created Chevalier du Tastevin, a Burgundian wine order. It happened something like this: we wanted our daughter, Jane, to learn French and a couple of Dijonnais wanted to reciprocate. Accordingly Andrée brought over her Thérèse, inspected us

Dr Slammer's Defiance of Jingle

and the house, decided we were all right and returned to Dijon. During the one day of Andrée's visit, the weather was appalling, pouring with rain and was so misty the garden was invisible. I tried to explain I was laying out a vineyard up the hill with the hope of producing enough wine to be self-sufficient. Well, one thing and another – my flourishing vineyard and Thérèse's obvious enjoyment – led us to Dijon to leave Jane, and to my election to Le Confrerie des Chevaliers du Tastevin – our host happened to be a giddy commandeur.

It also allowed me to give our hosts a dinner. I had heard about a hotel restaurant at Pont de Panet, some ten kilometres north of Dijon, which was new to our friends. Three days before the dinner I took Elizabeth my wife, daughter Jane and Winifred Saunders my bilingual secretary, to visit the establishment and organise the menu. Madame was delightful but clearly unimpressed by we English talking about food. However, when Winifred mentioned the Tastevin banquet, things changed dramatically. Madame left abruptly ("What on earth did you say to her, Winifred?") and re-appeared a few minutes later with a dusty bottle which she opened and dispensed liberally. True, in her excitement, she had shaken the bottle, but it was very lovely. "Oui?" Yes, indeed. So having settled the most important item – Gervrey Chambertin '47 – she was prepared to discuss the main course, and we were easily persuaded to have cailles étouffées – a brace of quail tied together and stuffed; and, before that, some local vegetables. "Et pour commencer?" Knowing the form now, I nodded: 'Oui, indeed, un vin blanc. Peut-être un Genevières," because our hosts' eldest daughter was born thereabouts. "Eh! c'est aimable – je suis très content!" So we were to start with a Meursault Genevières '61, and eat écrevisse à la nage (delicious fresh water prawns in and around a bowl of white wine) followed by truite à la crème. Whilst these mouth-watering arrangements were being noted, we were blissfully drinking Kir in the sunshine.

KIR   *1 teaspoon Cassis*
                                          1 wineglass white Burgundy
Put the cassis into a wineglass and top up with a dry white burgundy -
Aligote. It makes a delectable summer drink.
To make *KIR SUPREME* substitute a dry sparkling burgundy.

The dinner was even better than expected, turning into a riot - in
the Pickwickian sense. We finished up with cheese and local
strawberries, washed down by marc, prunelle and beer. By this time
the restaurant was full and I was remembering all the nursery songs
Mumsey had taught me - "savez vous planter les choux", "frère
Jacques", "sur le pont d'Avignon" and others. We not only sang
them, but acted them all over the dance floor - everybody in the
restaurant joining in. Oh, a great evening, proving conclusively
that wine improves the memory - if not overdone.
*"Wine in moderation - not in excess, for that makes men ugly - has
a thousand pleasant influences. It brightens the eye, improves the
voice, imparts a new vivacity to one's thoughts and conversation".*
La Ceremonie d'Intronisation des Chevaliers took place on the last
day of our stay, dans la Cuverie de Château de clos de Vougeot; we
were to be there by 6.30 pm. After six courses and five wines,
speeches and songs between, followed by coffee and le vieux marc,
it was 10.30 when our host gathered us together to drink
champagne in the Officers' disrobing room. A memorable evening
which finished about 4.30.

CHAMPAGNE COCKTAIL   *lump sugar*
                        Angostura
                        brandy
                        champagne
Into a small wine glass put the sugar soaked with Angostura. Cover with
brandy and gently fill with champagne.

During our stay in Burgundy I had been much involved with
tasting. You must realise my tasting is always for pleasure. I have
little ability to taste wine in the professional way, but I do enjoy

drinking wine, and une cave is conducive to pleasant drinking. The car too was happy – it was able to direct itself with exactitude along the Route des Grands Crux.

Amongst the many people I met in France, the greatest was Louis Latour, who conducted me to his village of Corton and to his caves in the old stone quarry. He gave us lunch in the delightful Restaurant du Marché in Beaune and took us back to his chateau to meet his family. I had the honour and great pleasure of being allowed to sign his old French edition of David Copperfield.

Two others, Père Remoissenet and Fils, Roland, were adamant they aged their wines as of old. There were only five or so growers left who did this and even this number was decreasing. Roland took me to another's cellar where we tasted several old wines. He explained at some length why it wasn't as good – by comparison.

"Bottle of wine to the gentleman on the box".

We were driven to Nantoux to see Thérèse's parents cottage which was being completely rebuilt. So far only the cellar had been renovated and we witnessed a barrel of wine being ceremoniously rolled in. Only then could the rest of the alterations be made. Nantoux is a tiny community with a vast old farmhouse at its centre and vineyards all round. Picking had started and all hands were at work. Granny was alone in the homestead, responsible for the food and drink. The jolly old farmer gave us a bottle of "vin douce" – grape juice which had started to ferment, which was working like mad with the pips popping up and down. It was only two days old, and a delicious thirst-quencher. Our host proclaimed it too young! He preferred it four days old when it was less sugary. After the grapes the walnuts would be harvested – everyone helping to pick each others' trees. What a happy life; but how I wished I could speak French.

Whilst in Burgundy I determined to buy a barrel of wine. Everything was to cost as little as possible on this experimental run.

Eventually I bought a Beaujolais from Coron Père et Fils and had it shipped in a second-hand barrel. I remember the excitement of hearing of its arrival in England, and, eventually, that it had been cleared by customs. Finally, it was laid to rest about a foot above the ground in an old oast house belonging to a neighbouring farmer. It had to be topped up with eighteen bottles of strong wine, which seemed a pretty good indication that someone had had a superb orgy somewhere between Dijon and Kent. I had visions of a carousal in the customs sheds. *The late Mr Bardell, after enjoying for many years the esteem and confidence of his sovereign, as one of the guardians of his royal revenues, glided almost imperceptibly from the world, to seek elsewhere for that repose and peace which a customs-house can never afford.*

So, according to Serjeant Buzfuz, they were at it even then. In fact, Mr Bardell had been knocked on the head with a quart-pot in a public house cellar.

After a few weeks I organised a bottling party – highly recommended, especially in an old oast house. It went something like this. Two people lay on the ground siphoning the wine into bottles ensuring that they were full to the brim. The first inch or so from each was poured into glasses and the bottles were corked using a primitive box-wood contraption and a mallet. They were then capped and stored – for a short time – and consumed incredibly quickly.

The importance of filling the bottles to the top is apparent. I suppose that by the end of the barrel, which produced 300 bottles, we, the serious workers, had drunk more than three bottles each. We were, in short, delightfully happy; despite a very sore hand as a result of that dastardly corking gadget. How simple now with my antique contraption!

One day I will import another barrel. It will be a new one, containing the best possible wine I can afford, and will be definitely only part of a larger consignment, travelling and being cleared through customs under surveillance.

My great-grandfather would have done it so easily. Many, many years ago, in a small town on the Mediterranean far from Naples, he met by intent an inn-keeper whose life had been saved by a generous and noble Englishman. As a result he found himself the guardian of one of those immense bottles in which the Italian peasants store their wine – a bottle holding some half dozen gallons

Miss Pross and Mr Cruncher buy wine

- bound round with basket work for greater safety on the journey. Yes, he had promised to deliver it to the noble Englishman. Read about the appalling difficulties of getting that corpulent bottle through Italy to Genoa in "The Italian Prisoner" - the topping up of my barrel was no irritation by comparison.

I have tasted wine in only a very few of the wineries round the world. In South Africa, near Stellenbosch, I stayed on the Blumberg estate. Father Blumberg, Simeon, and his dear wife Mary, brought up a large family of two sons and four daughters. As each reached the age of two, he or she was made a member of the board and was obliged to attend the monthly meetings. They were

all encouraged to talk - about the subject in hand if possible - and
listen. At the end of each item on the agenda, Simeon would thank
them and then TELL them what he intended. But what a nice
family. I have been lucky enough to see five of them in action in
that old Pickwickian Tavern, The George and Vulture. More
appropriately, they made excellent wines, started Cash and Carry
Wine shops and bought Bertrams, makers of the famous Van de
Hum (literally, Mr whats-his-name, because the Dutch settlers had
forgotten the name of the man who first made their beloved
Curacao.)
They have since sold the winery; but in England their wine
company, Robert James, has celebrated its 150th anniversary, and
their cash and carry wine shop is going great guns.
Australia produces some excellent wines. The Hunter Valley in
New South Wales is famous and there I met Murray Tyrell, one of
the few independent growers. It was pouring with rain and he
hadn't been able to start picking. Bored, he showed me round
himself, and we shared my pot of Stilton cheese to his obvious
enjoyment. With each successive Bath Oliver biscuit and Stilton, he
ordered up another and even better bottle from his private bin.
South Australia too produces good wines, both in the South of
Australia Vineyards (where I saw, of joy, the home of Emu Wines)
and in the Barossa valley where I toured Wyndham Hill Smith's
Yalumba estate (on which my son, John, worked for a short time),
and then ate yabbies at Orlando's Weinkeller. We spent an extra
day in Adelaide - the day predicted for its demise by earthquake,
fire and tidal wave by a mad house painter who had skipped it to
South Africa. His prophesy was taken seriously by many people
- some leaving everything and others towing boats to high
mountains. The Premier paddled on the foreshore, whilst we had a
long session in the Dickens bar of the Feathers, followed by an
excellent meal at that delightful restaurant, Maggies. She is worth
meeting, is Maggie Perkins. Needless to say Adelaide still stands.
When in Sydney I always visit another old friend, Don McWilliam.
The family is among the biggest growers and shippers in Australia
and now has large holdings in New Zealand. When last in New

SAUTERNE CHABLIS   *The rind of a Lemon*
or MOSELLE CUP   *6 good Sized Lumps of Sugar*
(Auntie Georgie)   *a little hot water*
Without Soda water   *a Tumbler full of Sherry*
Let this stand until the sugar is melted. Then stir well and add –
1 bottle Wine – stir again and put in Ice – in large lumps – *not too much.*
Very little Borage.

CLARET CUP   *the rind of a lemon*
(Auntie Georgie)   *6 good-sized lumps of sugar*
The ultimate –   *a bottle of hot water*
A better claret cup with   **a wine glass of brandy*
or without soda water   *1 bottle claret*
    2 good slices lemon
    a little nutmeg
    a very little borage
*Better still instead of a wine glass of brandy ¾ of a wine glass of curacao
– the glass being filled up with brandy. In this case 4 good-sized lumps of
sugar are sufficient – and a bottle of soda water may be added.

Put into large bowl the rind of a lemon, sugar lumps, water and brandy.
Let stand until sugar is melted, stir well and add the claret, slices of
lemon and nutmeg. Stir well and add plenty of ice in large lumps.
Finally add the borage.

"MAY DRINK"
(Auntie Georgie)
Take a handful of Woodroff – put it into a bowl with May or frottle of
Strawberries (or some slices of oranges or Pine Apple according to the
season) and half a pound of sugar, add a bottle of Rhine Wine, cover it
closely. Let it stand for a few hours and before serving it add another
bottle of Rhine Wine and half a bottle of Seltzer water. Also more Sugar
if you do not think it sweet enough.
The bowl to be iced.

Zealand I had a very pressing invitation to join them in conference
in Hastings – I wisely resisted the temptation.
Champagne is a wonderful preventative for "jet-lag". I have
travelled as far as New Zealand and been able to carry on, as
though I had merely taken an underground journey across London.

A bottle of champagne before boarding the aircraft – necessary to
counteract the effect of being penned up like sheep in the modern
airport – and thereafter a quarter of a bottle every hour on the
hour. Take it medicinally: sip it walking up and down the alleyway,
then sit back and relax for the next forty-five minutes. BUT, and
this is very important, no solid food must pass your lips. Your
tummy is largely responsible for the jeg-lag effect. So confuse it by
foreclosing on the food and shoot it down a regular drop of
medicine once an hour.

*Mr Tupman returned to his companions; and in another hour had
drowned all present recollection of Mr Alfred Jingle in an
exhilarating quadrille and a bottle of champagne.*

BUCKS FIZZ   *Champagne*
                                 Fresh orange juice
Fill a medium-sized goblet with half fresh orange juice and half
champagne. Bucks Fizz can be drunk at any time of the day – or night.
Grand for breakfast with a kipper grilled on the barbeque.

COMPOUND AND OTHER DRINKS

The story would be incomplete without some of the other drinks of
those times. They have glorious names and taste even better than
they sound. Many come from America which Charles Dickens

visited in 1842, and again in 1867-8. Some are very English and others are known on both sides of the Atlantic.

I have given a simple description of each, and, where possible, a recipe. Sometimes the names of my recipes may be misleading; these are family names, and I can't see my way to change them.

COBBLER

A long drink of wine, sugar and citrus juice, served with lots of crushed ice in large goblets, decorated with berries, fresh fruit and, if desired, a sprig of mint. Drink through straws.

> *CHAMPAGNE COBBLER*
> *1 teaspoon strained lemon juice*
> *1 teaspoon orange brandy*
> *champagne*
> *ice*
> *1 slice orange*

Put the lemon juice and orange brandy into a tumbler. Add a little ice and fill with the champagne. Stir gently and decorate with a slice of orange.

COLLINS

Tall cool drinks belonging to the punch family. Any basic spirit and the juice of a lemon or lime over ice cubes in a frosted high-ball glass, with sugar to taste and filled with soda, decorated with a slice of lemon and a cherry. They should be drunk through straws.

> *TOM COLLINS*
> *juice of ½ lemon*
> *1 teaspoon powdered sugar*
> *2 oz dry gin*
> *soda water*
> *2 dashes Angostura*

Shake well the lemon juice, sugar and gin with ice and strain into glass with a little more ice. Fill with soda water and top with two dashes of Angostura.

Decorate with slice of lemon, orange and cherry. Serve with straws.

COOLER

Another warm weather drink of the punch family, but with little or no lemon or lime juice – only the rind is used.

RUM COOLER   *½ teaspoon castor sugar*
                                2 oz rum
                                soda water
                                lemon peel
                                ice

Put the sugar and a little soda water into glass. Stir and add the ice and rum. Fill with soda and decorate with a spiral of lemon peel over the edge of the glass.

CUP

Wine, cider or a base spirit with brandy or curacao. A good party drink garnished with fruit in season. Delectable. The varieties are endless and can be dreamt up on the spur of the moment as the drink cupboard dictates. There are certain simple rules to follow: place the fruit in a bowl with the spirit, cover and leave for at least half an hour with the sugar. Then add the chosen liquor, ice and soda. Stir and serve. I start the brew reasonably strong – perhaps adding an ostentatious bottle of bubbly – and gradually weaken it. Everyone appreciates this next morning.

BISHOP'S CUP   *1 liqueur glass Orange Brandy*
                                 1 bottle Bishop (See page 55)
                                 1 bottle sparkling white wine
                                 1 bottle soda water
                                 1 orange
                                 ice

Cut three slices of the orange into a basin and squeeze the remainder of the juice into the basin together with the Orange Brandy and Bishop. Leave for half an hour and then add twelve ice cubes and the bottle of soda. Finally, just before serving, add the sparkling white wine.

CIDER CUP II   *2 large lumps sugar*
Amended from Auntie Georgie *1 wine glass medium sherry*
                                   ½ wine glass brandy
                                   ½ pint medium cider
                                   lemon peel
                                   dash Angostura
                                   ice

Put one lump sugar soaked with Angostura into pint tankard. Add the
second lump and the brandy. Then add the sherry, ice and cider,
squeezing the lemon peel on top.

CHAMPAGNE CUP   *4 or 5 large lumps of sugar*
(Auntie Georgie)   *the rind of a good lemon*
                                   pared very thin
                                   ice
                                   a good tumbler full of sherry
                                   a bottle of champagne
                                   a bottle of soda water

PEACH CUP   *2 firm ripe peaches*
                                   2 tablespoons castor sugar
                                   2 bottles still moselle
                                   1 bottle sparkling moselle

Using a silver knife peel one or two fine, ripe peaches and cut into small
pieces, losing as little juice as possible.
Place in a glass bowl and sprinkle with the sugar. Add sufficient light
Moselle to cover and allow to stand for half an hour to draw.
Add the remainder of the still wine stirring gently and sweeten to taste.
It is important to keep the bowl covered.
Just before serving add the bottle of sparkling Moselle very cold.
Keep the bowl on a bed of ice. On no account put ice into this cup.
Any white wine will do, but use a sparkling wine from the same region.
Strawberries or pineapple can be substituted for the peaches.

EGGNOG

An agreeable way of taking whole eggs with milk and nutmeg.
Greatly enjoyed in America.

WHISKEY EGGNOG   *1 fresh egg*
                       2 oz Southern Comfort
                       8 oz milk
                       ice
                       a little sugar
Shake all the ingredients well, and pour into a glass. Sprinkle with
nutmeg.

FIZZ

Early morning, mid-afternoon or evening pleasure. Any base spirit
with citrus fruit juice and sugar, shaken with ice, strained into a
wine glass and filled with fizz (soda water) or, exquisitely, a
sparkling white wine. It makes a grand breakfast with a kippered
herring grilled in the open over charcoal.

CHERRY BRANDY FIZZ   *juice of ½ lemon*
                       1 teaspoon castor sugar
                       2 oz Cherry Brandy
                       soda water
                       ice
Shake the lemon juice, sugar and Cherry Brandy with ice. Pour into an
eight oz glass, fill with soda and stir. Decorate with slice of lemon and
brandied cherries.

ORANGE FIZZ
Half a tot of orange brandy topped up with grapefuit juice and a splash
of soda makes an excellent drink, enjoyed especially by girls who like
Scotch. A dash of Angostura and ice enhance it.

FLIP

In England it was a mixture of cyder or beer and spirit, sweetened and heated with a hot poker. In America, a mixture of eggnog and fizz.

Every man put down his sixpence for a can of flip, which grateful beverage was brewed with all despatch, and set down in the midst of them on the brick floor; both that it might simmer and stew before the fire, and that its fragrant steam, rising up among them and mixing with the wreaths of vapour from their pipes, might shroud them in a delicious atmosphere of their own, and shut out all the world.

> *FLIP*
> To prepare Flip use equal measures of rough cider (scrumpy) and brandy with a pinch each of cinnamon, clove and ginger. Heat in a muller or in the tankard with a red-hot poker.
> Serve in small tankards with nutmeg grated atop.

JULEP

In England a sweet drink, especially a vehicle for medicine. But in Kentucky, a glorious drink made from bourbon whiskey and mint.

> *MINT JULEP*   *powdered sugar*
> *(For two strong, or*   *large mint leaves and sprigs*
> *four plain mortals)*   *1 bottle Bourbon*
>   *crushed ice*
>
> Leave favourite tankards, silver teaspoons and a bottle of Bourbon in the freezer for twenty-four hours. Remove with gloves and place the tankards on several layers of newspaper.
> Into each put five mint leaves, a little powdered sugar and a teaspoon of water. Now muddle (or bruise or whatever) and fill with crushed ice.
> Fill with Bourbon and stir hard to produce frost on the outside.
> Add more Bourbon, the sprig of mint dusted with a little sugar and drink through short straws with nose in the mint.
> Carry on filling tankards with more ice and Bourbon.

PUNCH (HOT)

"There is nothing like hot punch."

A drink usually of wine or spirit mixed with hot water or milk, and sugar, lemons and spice.

And of course, medicinally magnificent: *"If ever hot punch did fail to act as a preventative, it was merely because the patient fell into the vulgar error of not taking enough of it."*

A GEORGE AND VULTURE *Juice of 8 sweet oranges*
RECIPE FOR PUNCH *1 Bottle of Whisky*
1 Pint of Sherry
1 Quartern of Brandy
1½ pints of china tea
Nutmeg to cover a 1/-
Loaf sugar to sweeten
Rind of a lemon
Cinnamon if desired

This old recipe might have been tasted by Mr Pickwick and Sam Weller when they were "suspended" at the George and Vulture. It should be made hot in earthenware.

PUNCH (COLD)

"What did he say his name was?" "Punch, I think Sir."

RUM PUNCH

An old and golden rule when compounding Rum Punch (punch is always compounded), is to use:

ONE of sour (slightly unripe limes)
TWO of sweet (syrup)
THREE of strong (a good, dark, strong rum)
FOUR of weak (crushed ice)

Stir and top with two dashes of Angosutra.

PLANTERS PUNCH   *3 teaspoons powdered sugar*
1 oz fresh lime juice
3 oz dark rum
2 dashes Angostura
nutmeg

Mix ingredients well (except nutmeg) and pour into glass filled with
crushed ice. Dust with nutmeg and serve with straws.

MILK PUNCH I	*Juice of 4 lemons*
(Bob Sawyer)	*Rind of 2 lemons*
	1 Pineapple sliced and pounded
	¼ lb white sugar dissolve in hot water
	1 cup strong tea
	6 cloves
	20 coriander seeds
	1 stick cinnamon
	1 pint brandy
	1 pint rum
	1 pint boiling water
	1 quart hot milk

With the exception of the juice of two lemons and the hot milk, put all
the ingredients into a clean demijohn – the rum and brandy to be added
last.
Cork this down to prevent evaporation and allow to steep for at least six
hours. Then add the juice of two lemons and the hot milk. Mix and
strain, pouring the muddy liquid back into the demijohn. Cork tightly
and leave in a dark place.
After four or five weeks the milk will have precipitated and the resultant
clear liquid can be siphoned into bottles.
Add a tot of brandy to each if it is to be kept.
It must be well iced for drinking.

MILK PUNCH II	*2 tots brandy*
	1 tot rum
	1 teaspoon sugar
	4 tots full cream milk
	nutmeg

Put all the ingredients, except the nutmeg, into a shaker with a lot of ice.
Shake well and serve with nutmeg grated on top.

PURL

Another mixture of gin and porter, with beer added. *"For the rest, both the tap and the parlour of the Six Jolly Fellowship Porters gave upon the river, and had red curtains matching the noses of the regular customers, and were provided with comfortable fireside tin utensils, like models of sugar-loaf hats, made in that shape that they might, with their pointed ends, seek out for themselves glowing nooks in the depths of the red coals, when they mulled your ale, or heated for you those delectable drinks, Purl, Flip and Dog's Nose. The first of these humming compounds was a specialty of the Porters."*

> *PURL*
> Fill a muller with equal measures of Guinness and strong ale heated with root ginger, poured into mugs with a tot of gin and with nutmeg grated on top.

RICKEY

Cross between a Collins and a Sour, but lime juice is an essential ingredient – fresh.

> *GIN RICKEY*
> Put the juice of half a lime add the empty skin of that half lime into a glass with ice and two oz dry gin.
> Fill with soda water and serve with a stir rod.

ROCKY MOUNTAIN SNEEZER

Charles Dickens' New York landlord made him one to cure his catarrh. *"It appears to me to be compounded of all the spirits ever heard of in the world, with bitters, lemon, sugar, and snow. You can only make a true 'sneezer' when the snow is lying on the ground."*

ROCKY MOUNTAIN SNEEZER
Shake together two oz each of brandy and rum, with sugar and the juice
of a lemon and a handful of new snow – preferably from the Rocky
Mountains.
Add two dashes Angostura.

SANGAREE

A tall, sweet Old Fashioned without bitters, but with port floated
on top and nutmeg. In Spain, a cold drink of wine, diluted and
spiced, called Sangria.

PORT SANGAREE
Dissolve half a teaspoon castor sugar in one teaspoon water. Add two oz
port and two lumps of ice. Serve in an eight oz glass nearly filling with
soda water.
Stir and float a tablespoon brandy with a dusting of nutmeg.

SHRUB

Dickens usually refers to it as "srub". Lemon juice, Seville orange
juice, the finest Jamaica rum and sweets from good sugar-loaf make
the real srub.
At the swarry of the footmen of Bath, *the gentleman in blue, and
the man in orange, who were the chief exquisites of the party,
ordered 'cold srub and water'.*

SHRUB I   *½ gallon rum*
                                 ¾ pint orange juice
                                 ½ pint lemon juice
                                 peel of two lemons
                                 2 lbs loaf sugar
Slice lemon peel very thinly and put it with the fruit juice and spirit in a
large covered jar. Let it stand for two days, then pour over it the water in
which the sugar has been dissolved. Take out the lemon peel and leave
for twelve days before using.

SHRUB II   *½ lb strained Seville orange juice*
                                    2 lbs crystal sugar
                                    3 pints rum or brandy
Dissolve sugar in cold orange juice and blend with spirit. Strain through
a jelly bag. Bottle and cork.

SLING

A long drink made with spirit, bitters and soda water. Pimms
claims to be the original Sling – No 1 being gin based.

GIN SLING   *3 oz gin*
                                    1 oz sweet vermouth
                                    2 dashes Angostura
                                    lemonade
                                    soda water
                                    ice
Into a pint glass tankard, put the gin, vermouth and Angostura. Top up
with lemonade and soda. Add ice and decorate with a slice of apple,
orange and lemon and small thin cucumber rind. Top with a sprig of
borage with a dash of orange bitters, if available.

SOUR

A highly concentrated punch decorated with a slice of lemon and a
cherry.

WHISKY SOUR   *juice of ½ lemon*
                                    1 teaspoon castor sugar
                                    2 dashes Angostura
                                    2 oz Scotch whisky
                                    ice
Shake all the ingredients with the ice and strain into glass allowing a little
ice to fall into the glass. Decorate with half a slice of lemon and a cherry.

SPRUCE

The Magpie and Stump in Clare Market, London, boasted that it stocked Dantzig spruce; a beer made from the extract of the leaves and branches of the spruce fir.

SWIZZLE

A tall cool drink of lime, sugar, liquor and bitters packed with crushed ice; originally from the West Indies and therefore traditionally made from rum.

Despite sampling Green Swizzles for nearly fifty years, I have not succeeded in recreating that subtle flavour last savoured in Barbados. However, the recipe below is well worth trying. In the land of their origin, they say Swizzles should be downed, not sipped. Without denying the rightful glamour of the Swizzle, it is only right to warn the uninitiated of the apparent gentleness of this disarming drink. It has an artful way of springing surprises.

GREEN SWIZZLE

2 oz rum
1 teaspoon creme de menthe
juice of a lime
1 teaspoon castor sugar
2 dashes Angostura
ice
Soda water

Shake the ingredients except for the soda, and pour into glass with some of the ice. Top up with soda. It should be stirred by the drinker with a swizzle stick - a four or five branched stick of West Indian wormwood.

TODDY

Sweetened drink of spirits, hot water, clove, nutmeg, cinnamon and lemon peel. This simplified recipe comes from my grandmother, Mumsey, to be drunk medicinally.

WHISKY TODDY   *juice of a lemon*
                       1 tablespoon brown sugar
                       1 tablespoon honey
                       1 large tot whisky
                       boiling water

Into a heat-resisting tumbler put the juice of a lemon, the brown sugar
and honey. Three quarters fill with boiling water and stir well. Fill with
whisky and drink as hot as possible.

WASSAIL

A festive occasion, a drinking bout, or a kind of liquor drunk on
these occasions.

*"It was high time to make the wassail now; therfore I had up the
materials (which, together with their proportions and combinations,
I must decline to impart, as the only secret of my own I was ever
known to keep,) and made a glorious jorum."*

WIMMEL

An excellent digestive which tends to encourage talk.

WIMMEL
A kummel taken as a digestive is excellent, but even better if ten drops of
scotch whisky are added – enough to make it straw coloured.

Threepenn'orth Rum

Some Drinkers in Dickens

Those were drinking days, and most men drank hard. Thus observed Charles Dickens in A Tale of Two Cities during the French Revolution. It was still the same in his day.

I had planned to write about DRINKERS in Dickens, but very quickly changed my mind; especially when Alan Watts, Hon. Secretary of The Dickens Fellowship, commented casually that you could open any early book at random and find a drinker. It isn't exactly like that, but very nearly. And so this chapter covers but a few of those drinkers – there are plenty more where they come from, and I can recommend dedicating many a happy hour to finding them and comparing them with this choice.

The difficulty has been to omit people, and to know how best to categorise those chosen. I have divided them into six classes:

Drunkards, who can't help themselves.

Desperate drinkers, the rough types and hypocrites.

Medicinal drinkers, who must have an excuse to drink.

Good drinkers, who drink hard and can take it.

Drinkers like you and I, who enjoy its conviviality.

And, finally, the *Sowers of wild oats,* those getting experience.

Dickens himself was a drinker, but a temperate one. He once was a sower of wild oats, as was David Copperfield, went through the drinker stage like Mr Pickwick, and ended by drinking medicinally; but thankfully not like those worthy women, Mrs Gamp and Mrs Crupp. Towards the end of his life, an egg beaten up in sherry or champagne was his medicine, especially for sustaining him during his public readings.

I hope to whet your appetite, to encourage you to re-read the books to find even greater characters. Dickens populated his world with real people, perhaps a shade larger than life; nevertheless they live as much today as they did a hundred years ago and more.

DRUNKARDS

MAYPOLE HUGH

The whole Barnaby Rudge crew, especially *Maypole Hugh*. *"Will this man drink?"* *"Drink! He'd drink the Thames up, if it was strong enough"*.

SYDNEY CARTON

Sydney Carton, clearly a drunkard, *idlest and most umpromising of men, was Stryver's great ally. What the two drank together, between Hilary Term and Michaelmas, might have floated a king's ship.* But he spoils it by dying on the guillotine, by taking the place of the husband of the girl he loves: *"It is a far, far better thing that I do than I have ever done; it is a far, far better rest that I go to than I have ever known."*

MR WICKFIELD

Mr Wickfield becomes a real drunkard through the wiles of the villainous Uriah Heep: *"The old ass has drunk himself into a state of dotage."* But when Mr Micawber uncharacteristically unmasks him, Mr Wickfield is gently brought back to life by that angel, Agnes, his daughter and the second Mrs Copperfield.

KROOK

Krook, a dealer in rags and bones, "Old Boguey", was so much under the influence of raw gin, of which he drank in great quantities that he died of *Spontaneous Combustion, and none other of all the deaths that can be died.*

MR DOLLS

But for me, the most depraved drunkard is *Mr Dolls*. He had been a good workman at his trade, but was weak and trembling, falling to pieces, and never sober. What gives him the prize, is that he betrayed his own daughter, Jenny Wren, his sharp little "parent", for sixty three-pennyworths of rum. And again, after that, *Mr Dolls, accepting the shilling, promptly laid it out in two threepennyworths of conspiracy against his life, and two threepennyworths of raging repentance.* Stumblingly pursuing these two designs – they both meant rum, the only meaning of which he was capable – he ended up a harmless bundle of torn rags on a stretcher.

DESPERATE DRINKERS

DANIEL QUILP

Daniel Quilp, the dwarf money-lender and dealer in second-hand ships' fittings. Remember his drinking with Dick Swiveller on page 39? And his insidious menacing of Mrs Quilp: *"If you ever listen to those beldames again, I'll bite you." With this laconic threat, which he accompanied with a snarl that gave him the appearance of being particularly in earnest, Mr Quilp bade her clear the tea-board away, and bring the rum. The spirit being set before him in a huge case-bottle, which had originally come out of some ship's locker, he ordered cold water and a box of cigars; and these being supplied, the small lord of creation took his first cigar and mixed his first glass of grog.*

MR PECKSNIFF

Mr Pecksniff, the greatest of hypocrites who inspired the word Pecksniffian to indicate – just that. *Having swallowed his share of*

Tony Weller ejects Mr Stiggins

the enlivening fluid, Mr Pecksniff, under pretence of going to see if the coach were ready, went secretly to the bar, and had his own little bottle filled, in order that he might refresh himself at leisure in the dark coach without being observed.

MR STIGGINS

Mr Stiggins, must come into this category. Tony Weller relates the circumstances of the second Mrs Weller's death from an overdose of Stiggins: *"I am wery sorry to have the pleasure of bein a Bear of ill news your Mother in law cort cold consekens of imprudently settin too long on the damp grass in the rain a hearin of a shepherd who warnt able to leave off till late at night owen to his havin vound his-self up vith brandy and vater and not being able to stop his-self till he got a little sober which took a many hours to do the doctor says if she'd svallo'd varm brandy and vater artervards insted of afore she mightn't have been no vus"*

FANG

Fang, the bullying magistrate, whose *face was stern, and much flushed. If he were really not in the habit of drinking rather more than was exactly good for him, he might have brought an action against his countenance for libel, and recovered heavy damages.*

MR SNEVELLICCI

Mr Snevellicci, was scented with rum and water. *Most public characters have their failings; and the truth is that Mr Snevellicci was a little addicted to drinking; or, if the whole truth must be told, that he was scarcely ever sober. He knew in his cups three distinct stages of intoxication, - the dignified - the quarrelsome - the amorous. When professionally engaged he never got beyond the dignified; in private circles he went through all three, passing from one to another with a rapidity of transition often rather perplexing to those who had not the honour of his acquaintance.*

SARAH GAMP

My star choice must be *Sarah Gamp,* who gives so many pearls of wisdom, no less than the word Gamp itself. They are scattered through this little book. Think of her saying so sincerely: *"If it wasn't for the nerve a little sip of liquor gives me (I never was able to do more than taste it), I never could go through with what I sometimes has to do."*

Mrs Harris was surprised that Mrs Gamp *"could sick-nurse and monthly likewise, on the little that you takes to drink."*

In her drinking too, she was very punctual and particular, requiring a pint of mild porter at lunch, a pint at dinner, half-a-pint as a species of stay or holdfast between dinner and tea, and a pint of the celebrated staggering ale, or Real Old Brighton Tipper, at supper; besides the bottle on the chimney-piece.

"If they draws the Brighton Tipper here, I take that ale at night, my love; it being considered wakeful by the doctor."

"But now my half pint of porter fully satisfies; perwisin', Mrs Harris, that it is brought reg'lar, and draw'd mild – but I am but a poor woman, and I earns my living hard; and therefore I DO require it, which I makes confession, to be brought reg'lar and draw'd mild."

If Mrs Gamp finds her half pint of porter settling heavy on her chest she knows she is indisposged.

What riches!

MEDICINAL DRINKERS

Mrs Gamp might have felt happier here: In fact she could appear almost anywhere in these pages – and does. However, she has already been a star, *and, possessing herself of the bottle and glass, has proved to be very choice in her drinking: She was very punctual and particular, besides the bottle on the chimley-piece.*

MRS PETOWKER

Mrs Petowker, when she was to be married, made use of the medicinal properties of brandy and was supported through the preparatory robing, by *strong tea and brandy in alternate doses as a means of strengthening her feeble limbs and causing her to walk steadier.*

MRS BLOSS

Mrs Bloss, when fatigued, had *a mutton chop, pickle, a pill, a pint bottle of stout and other medicines carried upstairs.* She took her pill with a draught of Guinness.

OUR BORE

Our Bore was successfully treated by physician Jilkins by the prescribing of a mutton chop with a glass of the finest old sherry on the first day, followed by two mutton chops and two glasses of the finest old sherry the next day and so on for a week!

MRS CRUPP

Mrs Crupp, however, wins my award. She was David Copperfield's landlady, and was a martyr to a curious disorder called "the spazzums", which was generally accompanied with inflammation of the nose, and required to be constantly treated with peppermint. Not only did she suffer from "spazzums" but was a woman of penetration: she knew immediately that David was in love because he crammed his feet into the smallest shoes. *She came up to me one evening, when I was very low, to ask if I could oblige her with a little tincture of cardamums mixed with rhubarb, and flavoured with seven drops of the essence of cloves, which was the best remedy for her complaint; – or, if I had not such a thing by me, with a little brandy, which was the next best. It was not, she remarked, so palatable to her, but it was the next best.*

GOOD DRINKERS

GRIP

Grip drew fifty corks at least which made a great impression on the magistrate's mind. *A country gentleman of the true school. He was in the commission of the peace, and could write his name almost legibly; could eat more solid food, drink more strong wine, go to bed every night more drunk and get up every morning more sober, than any man in the county.*

BOB SAWYER

Bob Sawyer drank hard, but then medical students had to. He enjoyed himself almost furiously, unlike his friend, Ben Allen, who fast relapsed into the sentimental and insensible. He compounded the Milk Punch for the coach journey between Bristol and Birmingham in 1828 - the recipe has luckily been handed down from generation to generation. *"But what will you take? Do as we do?"* And a black bottle half full of brandy was produced. *"You don't take water, of course?"*
"Thank you," replied Mr Winkle. "It's rather early. I should like to qualify it, if you have no objection."
"None in the least, if you can reconcile it to your conscience," replied Bob Sawyer; tossing off, as he spoke, a glass of the liquor with great relish.

ALFRED JINGLE

Alfred Jingle who was always about a bottle and a half ahead of his companions, not that they were well known for the strength of their heads. *He emptied his glass, which he had filled about two minutes before, and poured out another, with the air of a man who was used to it.*

Conviviality at Bob Sawyer's

JEREMIAH FLINTWINCH

Jeremiah Flintwinch was far too seasoned a drinker for M. Blandois. He had at the end of the third bottle of port wine *the appearance of a perfect ability to go on all night; or, if occasion were, all next day, and all next night.*

SAM WELLER

Sam Weller himself, whose powers of suction, according to his father, would *"ha' made an uncommon fine oyster, Sammy, if you'd been born in that station o' life."*

THE BAGMAN'S UNCLE

The Bagman's Uncle beats them all. What a man! Let that one-eyed Bagman tell you. *"He collected for Tiggin and Welps and his great journey was in the fall of the leaf going from London to Edinburgh, from Edinburgh to Glasgow, from Glasgow back to Edinburgh and thence to London by smack. You are to understand that this second visit to Edinburgh was for his own pleasure. He used to go back for a week, just to look up his old friends; and what with breakfasting with this one, lunching with that, dining with a third, and supping with another, a pretty tight week he used to make of it. I don't know whether any of you, gentlemen, ever partook of a real substantial hospitable Scotch breakfast, and then went out to a slight lunch of a bushel of oysters, a dozen or so of bottled ale, and a noggin or two of whisky to close up with. If you ever did, you will agree with me that it requires a pretty strong head to go out to dinner and supper afterwards.*

But, bless your hearts and eyebrows, all this sort of thing was nothing to my uncle! He was so well seasoned, that it was mere child's play. I have heard him say that he could see the Dundee people out, any day, and walk home afterwards without staggering. One night, within four-and-twenty hours of the time when he had settled to take shipping for London, my uncle supped at the house of a very old friend of his, a Bailie Mac something and four syllables after it, who lived in the old town of Edinburgh. I don't quite recollect how many tumblers of whisky toddy each man drank after supper; but this I know, that about one o'clock in the morning, the bailie's grown-up son became insensible while attempting the first verse of "Willie brewed a peck o' maut;" and he having been, for half-an-hour before, the only other man visible above the mahogany, it occured to my uncle that it was almost time to think about going: especially as drinking had set in at seven o'clock, in order that he might get home at a decent hour. But, thinking it might not be quite polite to go just then, my uncle voted himself into the chair, mixed another glass, rose to propose his own health, addressed himself in a neat and complimentary speech, and drank the toast with great enthusiasm. Still nobody woke; so my uncle took a little drop more - neat this time, to prevent the toddy from disagreeing with him - and, laying violent hands on his hat, sallied forth into the street." It was a wild and gusty night, and his uncle walked the best part of a mile and came to a waste piece of ground with old worn-out mail coaches on it. To cut a long story short, they all came to life at two o'clock in the morning, and my uncle got involved in a melodramatic night, giving his oath to a lovely but ghostly girl that he would never marry anyone else. He never did; refusing several eligible landladies on her account and dying a bachelor at last.

DRINKERS

MR PICKWICK

Most drinkers in Dickens drink to give pleasure. *Mr Pickwick* does and he certainly enjoys life: *The mistletoe had just been suspended, and this same branch instantaneously gave rise to a scene of general and most delightful struggling and confusion; in the midst of*

Mr Pickwick and his Friends under the influence of Salmon

which, Mr Pickwick, with a gallantry which would have done honour to a descendent of Lady Tollimglower herself, took the old lady by the hand, led her beneath the mystic branch, and saluted her in all courtesy and decorum; "we old folks must have a glass of wine together."

TONY WELLER

Tony Weller who, when he found Sam at the Blue Boar writing a Valentine, raised Sam's tumbler to his lips and drank off its contents in consequence of his feelings being too much for him; and followed it with *"a double glass o' the inwariable, my dear."*

GABRIEL VARDEN

Gabriel Varden, the locksmith, with his Toby jug: *"Put Toby this way, my dear." Applying his lips to the worthy old gentleman's benevolent forehead, the locksmith, kept them there so long, at the same time raising the vessel slowly in the air, that at length Toby stood on his head upon his nose, when he smacked his lips and set him on the table again with fond reluctance.*

CAPTAIN CUTTLE

Captain Cuttle who, *after taking a glass of warm rum-and-water, made a rush down the court, lest its good effects should evaporate. And, not to be bitter on a man who had done his duty, the captain whispered in Mr Perch's ear, that if he felt disposed for a glass of rum-and-water, and would follow, he would be happy to bestow the same upon him. When they were alone again, the captain insisted on Florence eating a slice of dry toast, and drinking a glass of spiced negus (which he made to perfection).*

MR MICAWBER

Mr Micawber must rank first, having, as I have, his blood in my veins. If ever he had an extra penny, he thought of all the friends he would have to a party. He loved the ceremony of compounding a glass of gin punch of an evening. However depressed, punch always enabled him to forget his troubles (see page 43), except on one occasion, when the cares of the world had really borne him down, even the lemons, and other appliances he used in making punch failed to take his mind off his desperate plight, and, David watched him *putting the lemon-peel into the kettle, the sugar into the snuffer-tray, the spirit into the empty jug, and confidently attempting to pour boiling water out of a candlestick.* And then the crisis came: *He clattered all his means and implements together, rose from his chair, pulled out his pocket-handkerchief and burst into tears.*

"My dear Copperfield" from behind his handkerchief, "this is an occupation, of all others, requiring an untroubled mind, and self-respect. I cannot perform it. It is out of the question!"

But that was the only time in his troubled life. Mostly he compounded the perfect drink. *"Punch, my dear Copperfield, like time and tide, waits for no man. Ah! it is at the present moment in high flavour. My love,* (to Mrs Micawber, who never did leave him) *will you give me your opinion?"*

SOWERS OF WILD OATS

DICK SWIVVLER

Dick Swivvler certainly. Remember his throwing away the neat schiedam offered by Quilp? (see page 39) I remember him for this: *"Fan the sinking flame of hilarity with the wing of friendship; and pass the rosey wine!"*

DAVID COPPERFIELD

But neither he, nor any of the others, reached the standard of *David Copperfield* – the last of my drinkers, he is the truest Sower.

I have sown in exactly the same manner, as I hope Charles did too. Can you remember your first dissipation? Remind yourself by re-

Mr Swiveller's Libation

reading David Copperfield, Chapter 24, *"I take too much to drink."*
It deserves to be quoted in full, but space prohibits it.

He has his first bachelor party soon after taking up lodgings with
Mrs Crupp. *"Everything was very good; we did not spare the
wine . . . I went on, by passing the wine faster and faster yet, and
continually starting up with a cockscrew to open more wine, long
before any was needed. I proposed Steerforth's health. I said he was
my dearest friend, the protector of my boyhood, and the
companion of my prime. I said I was delighted to propose his
health. I said I owed him more obligations than I could ever repay,
and held him in a higher admiration than I could ever express. I
finished by saying, 'I'll give you Steerforth! God bless him! Hurrah!'
We gave him three times three, and another, and a good one to
finish with. I broke my glass in going round the table to shake
hands with him, and I said (in two words) "Steerforth,
you'retheguidingstarofmyexistence.*

And later, *"somebody was leaning out of my bedroom window,
refreshing his forehead against the cool stone of the parapet, and
feeling the air upon his face. It was myself. I was addressing myself
as 'Copperfield', and saying 'Why did you try to smoke? You might
have known you couldn't do it.'*

*Steerforth then said, 'You are all right, Copperfield, are you not?'
and I told him, 'Neverberrer'."*

Still later, *"How somebody, lying in my bed, at cross purposes, in a
feverish dream all night – the bed a rocking sea, that was never still!
How, as that somebody slowly settled down into myself, did I begin
to parch, and feel as if my outer covering of skin were a hard board;
my tongue the bottom of an empty kettle, furred with long service,
and burning up over a slow fire; the palms of my hands, hot plates
of metal which no ice could cool!"*

Hints on Drinking

"What is the odds so long as the fire of soul is kindled at the taper of conwiviality, and the wing of friendship never moults a feather?"
If there is a message in this book, it is that drinking is for pleasure. Don't drink to get drunk in the quickest possible way and become insensible to those around. A good party should be savoured and remembered with pleasure – yes, even early next morning.
"In the Proverbs of Solomon you will find the following words, 'may we never want a friend in need, nor a bottle to give him'."
A party will be long remembered if the mix of people and drink are right: start with a strong drink and gradually weaken it; provide lots of appetising tit-bits. Your friends will bless you next morning when they wake bright-eyed and bushy-tailed and actually remember how nice your guests were and how splendid a host you were.
In the recipes, reference is made to Measures, Tots, Jiggers and Ounces, depending on the source or date of the particular recipe. Take two ounces (= two bar shots) as an average: if the recipe calls for a small measure use one ounce, if generous try three ounces. Individual tastes vary and as long as the proportions are clear, you can make the drink as strong or weak as you want. Spirits were devastatingly strong on those days: you will be using a spirit distilled to a purity unknown in the 1830's.
Many old recipes for hot drinks call for "toast" or "a brown toast". Tea was very expensive: toasted bread was put into a jug and boiling water poured over it and left for a time before straining off – Donkey Tea.
Mrs Micawber, that great optimist, said *"experientia does it – as*

papa used to say.'' Try anything. It is great fun and as long as the basic rules are kept, and if the result is weak (especially if you have drivers as guests), you won't poison them. Some people are desperately allergic to eggwhites, so with the exception of Long Life and Eggnog, they do not appear in the recipes. If the drink is rough, heat it or make it so cold it cannot be tasted. Is this why some people drink beer practically frozen? I have an American friend who likes his white wine with slivers of ice in it. If it hasn't, he adds a lump of ice: sacrilege. If you drink for pleasure, the smell and taste are important and must be distinctive.

There was a toothache in everything. The wine was so bitter cold that it forced a little scream from Miss Tox, which she had great difficulty in turning into a "Hem!"

Conclusion

Perhaps the most significant pronouncement made by my great-grandfather on the subject, appears in the rollicking story of the Baron of Grogzwig. The Baron asked the Genius of Despair and Suicide:

"Do you drink?"

"Nine times out of ten," came the reply, *"and then very hard."*

"Don't you ever drink in moderation?"

"No," replied the dread spirit with a shudder, *"that breeds cheerfulness."*

The Great Port Controversy

Mr Pickwick certainly confounded the scientific world with his theory of Tittlebats and when he traced to their source the mighty ponds of Hampstead; but it is as nothing compared to THE GREAT PORT CONTROVERSY started in those same Posthumous Papers of the Pickwick Club when Wilkins Flasher, Esquire, of the Stock Exchange, was talking to Mr Frank Simmery, also of the Stock Exchange in 1828 about a colleague, Mr Boffer, who had failed.

"I'm very sorry he has failed," said Wilkins Flasher, Esquire. "Capital dinners he gave."

"Fine port he had too," remarked Mr Simmery. "We are going to send our butler to the sale tomorrow, to pick up some of that sixty-four."

History alas does not relate what became of Mr Boffer, or whether Wilkins Flasher, Esquire, or Mr Simmery got that fine sixty-four port; but that little sentence about the 1764 port has given rise to so much heated argument among the port pundits of the world that it has become known as *The Great Port Controversy*.

It started seriously in the correspondence columns of The Sunday Times in 1961. Alastair Lucas quoted it and said that 1764 was another error of fact in Pickwick Papers. Certainly my great-grandfather did make mistakes in those early days. At that time he was finishing Pickwick Papers and was writing Oliver Twist – both in monthly parts – editing a monthly magazine and writing hundreds of letters.

The following week saw Warner Allen agreeing about the 1764 port and adding that merchants and shippers were fumbling with the shape of the bottle – a cylindrical one was necessary for binning away – and that the first bottle was dated 1770. I came across these cuttings in the archives of Dickens House and it seemed to me wrong to castigate Dickens for a gap of a mere six years. In any case vintage port didn't suddenly appear: it surely must have evolved.

Simply put, vintage port is a wine with brandy added at an early stage to check fermentation and preserve the natural sweetness of the grape. It is then kept in bottle for twelve to twenty years or more to allow it to get over this initial shock and to mature gently.

In fact brandy had been added long before the mid-18th century; but for a different reason. It was to fortify the finished wine for its long journey to England, and to produce the full-bodied wine enjoyed in those days.

Was it possible that the "Quality Control" went wrong? That the cellarman added the brandy far too early? He would be soundly rated for his mistake. But a pipe of port was valuable even in the 1850s, and so it was shipped along with the others. What a surprise, therefore, when that particular one was singled out as being far superior to the others! How was it produced? And then they discovered that the mistake was really a considerable achievement - a breakthrough, and no doubt other shippers practised a little early industrial espionage to find out how it had been done. It would have taken longer than a mere six years.

The cylindrical bottle was a bit of a red herring. George Robertson, one of the greater port pundits, knows a shipper who, certainly until very recently, matured his port in bottles standing up. Thus the shape of the bottle may not be so important. But even the cylindrical bottle didn't appear over night - it had to evolve. We know it was in common use for the first great vintage of 1775 and the first shipper to use it would be anxious to prevent his competitors getting it.

All in all it looked as though my great-grandfather was right. The early records are hazy - in fact are non-existent in Portugal where they were all destroyed during the Peninsular war.

And then John Davy suggested that he would invite some of those port pundits to a luncheon to debate this fascinating subject in the right surroundings. Thus it was that on 13 February 1980 in Mother Bunches, in London, were gathered together eleven charming and erudite experts who entered into the spirit of the great debate, and, after some four hours, admitted that the subject was of such profound importance it would be necessary to continue in some similar surroundings at a later date. At least two shippers were happy in the belief that it was their port which had found its way into Mr Boffer's cellar. Thus it was that Mr Dickens was vindicated.

Charles Dickens outside Gads Hill

Charles Dickens' Wine Cellar

Summary of the contents of the wine cellar at Gad's Hill
compiled from the Catalogue of the Sale, August 1870.

 4 dozen of Cyder
12 dozen of brown Sherry – a dry golden Sherry, shipped by C & G Ellis
18 bottles Sherry "Solera"
 1 dozen Sherry, very delicate – old dry pale Sherry "Preciosa", C & G Ellis
 1 dozen Amontillado
13 Magnums Golden Sherry, very old, full flavoured
 4 dozen rare old Madeira, bottled from a cask of Ellis, marked
    very rare "Rutherford"
 5 bottles Old Madeira (vintage 1818), very rare
 5 dozen Port, very dry and delicate, 22 years in bottle,
    Cockburn's shipping, C & G Ellis
 8 bottles Old Port, Ellis, and 1 ditto, Peters and Hall
18 Magnums Port, extra quality, vintage 1851, bottled 1854
 5 dozen of Port, vintage 1834, from Alderman Humphrey's Sale, March 1865
 2 bottles of Port, vintage 1820
16 dozen of Medoc, C & G Ellis
 2 dozen bottles of "La Rose". C & G Ellis
 3 dozen of "Chateaux Margaux", Bourjois
 5 dozen of "Leoville", Bourjois
13 bottles of "Chateau D'Issan" vintage 1858
 7 dozen "Bran Mouton" vintage 1858 from the Chateau, very choice
 1 dozen Magnums Claret, vintage 1858, high flavoured, very fine
 3 bottles of very fine East India Claret
16 bottles of Burgundy "Clos Vougeot"
16 bottles of Volnay

- 9   bottles of Chambertin
- 4   pint bottles of Old Lisborn
- 17   dozen champagne, Bouzy
- 8   dozen dry champagne, C & G Ellis
- 2   dozen sparkling Muscatel
- 2   dozen Moselle, "Kuperberg", C & G Ellis
- 30   bottles Stein
- 18   bottles Sauterne
- 30   bottles Australian wine, red and white
- 3   dozen bottles Hock "Johannisberg", imported from the Methernich vineyards for Mr Dickens
- 16   bottles still Moselle "Zullinger Schlossberg", vintage 1861
- 5   dozen "Chateau y Quen" Bourgois
- 2   dozen "Haut Sauterne", very fine, Bourgois
- 16   bottles of Lunel
- 13   dozen of Milk Punch, Ballard, Broadstairs
- 17   bottles of "Kirch Wassis" bought in the Black Forest in 1854
- 11   bottles of Eau D'Or
- 17   bottles of Curacoa
- 3   dozen of cordial Gin, Justerini and Brooks
- 5   dozen fine old Pine Apple Rum, C & G Ellis
- 9   dozen Dark Brandy, Henessy's shipping, 10 years old
- 18   dozen very fine old Pale Brandy, F Courvoisier & Co's shipping
- 17   dozen very fine old Highland Whiskey, Cockburn & Co., Leith
- 16   bottles of Old Hollandche Genever Hoboken de Brie and Tarlay

NOTES

GIN BASED CORDIALS

MADEIRA

PORT

RUM

SHERRY

120

SOME DRINKERS IN DICKENS

INDEX OF RECIPES

INDEX OF DRINKS, CURES AND PUBS

(references to recipes are shown in italics)

"when found make a note of"

<u>PURSERS PURGE</u>   1 Brandy
2 Dry Gin
1 Dash Angostura

Thoroughly mixed into a long glass with ice, and topped up with sparkling grapefruit juice.
Drink through straws.